BEST OF

New Orleans

Ryan Ver Berkmoes

Best of New Orleans
2nd edition – February 2005
First published – March 2003

Published by Lonely Planet Publications Pty Ltd
ABN 36 005 607 983

Australia   Head Office, Locked Bag 1, Footscray, Vic 3011
            ☎ 03 8379 8000 fax 03 8379 8111
            ⌨ talk2us@lonelyplanet.com.au
USA   150 Linden St, Oakland, CA 94607
            ☎ 510 893 8555 toll free 800 275 8555
            fax 510 893 8572
            ⌨ info@lonelyplanet.com
UK   72–82 Rosebery Avenue, London EC1R 4RW
            ☎ 020 7841 9000 fax 020 7841 9001
            ⌨ go@lonelyplanet.co.uk

This title was commissioned in Lonely Planet's Oakland
office and produced by: Commissioning Editor Jay Cooke
Coordinating Editor Cinzia Cavallaro Coordinating
Cartographer Emma McNicol Layout Designer John
Shippick Editors Carly Hall, Victoria Harrison Indexer
Carly Hall Cartographers Corey Hutchison, Kusnandar
Managing Cartographer Alison Lyall Cover Designer
Pepi Black Cover Artwork Wendy Wright Project
Manager Eoin Dunlevy Mapping Development Paul
Piaia Thanks to Martin Heng, Kerryn Burgess, Anthony
Phelan, Fiona Siseman, LPI, Adrianna Mammarella, Kate
McDonald, Celia Wood, Jane Hart

© Lonely Planet Publications Pty Ltd 2005.

All rights reserved.

Photographs by Lonely Planet Images and Ray Laskowitz
except for the following: p21 Richard Cummins, p35 Jerry
Alexander, p38 John Elk III, p54 Jerry Alexander, p58 Jerry
Alexander, p67 Richard Cummins, p79 Richard Cummins.
Cover photograph Wrought iron balcony detail in the
French Quarter, Cosmo Condina/Alamy Images. All images
are copyright of the photographers unless otherwise
indicated. Many of the images in this guide are available
for licensing from Lonely Planet Images: ⌨ www
.lonelyplanetimages.com

ISBN 1 74059 797 4

Printed by Markono Print Media Pte Ltd, Singapore

Lonely Planet and the Lonely Planet logo are trademarks
of Lonely Planet and are registered in the US Patent and
Trademark Office and in other countries.

Lonely Planet does not allow its name or logo to be
appropriated by commercial establishments, such as
retailers, restaurants or hotels. Please let us know of any
misuses: ⌨ www.lonelyplanet.com/ip

HOW TO USE THIS BOOK

Color-Coding & Maps

Each chapter has a color code along the
banner at the top of the page which is also
used for text and symbols on maps (eg all
venues reviewed in the Highlights chapter
are orange on the maps). The fold-out
maps inside the front and back covers are
numbered from 1 to 6. All sights and venues
in the text have map references; eg, (3, C3)
means Map 3, grid reference C3. See p96 for
map symbols.

Prices

When more than one price for an attraction
is listed in this book (eg $10/5), it reflects the
highest adult and the cheapest concession.
Concession prices can include senior, student
or child discounts. Meal cost and room rate
categories are listed at the start of the Eating
and Sleeping chapters, respectively.

Text Symbols

☎	telephone
⌧	address
⌨	email/website address
$	admission
☺	opening hours
ⓘ	information
⛫	streetcar
🚌	bus
🚗	car
P	parking available
♿	wheelchair access
⌧	on site/nearby eatery
☻	child-friendly venue
V	good vegetarian selection

Contents

From the Publisher

AUTHOR

Ryan Ver Berkmoes

Ryan Ver Berkmoes first visited New Orleans in 1986 on a weekend trip that would have been memorable if he could remember any of it. Since then, his trips there have spanned the calendar and have included grubbing on the ground for beads at Mardi Gras, bouncing off the ground at obscure all-night bars and plowing through plenty of grub at the city's dozens of fabulous eateries. He seriously wants to move there as it would cut down on airfare. Until then, he earns his beads living in the San Francisco Bay Area and writing about travel.

Paul McGinn first showed me New Orleans and through a fabulous convergence of the planets joined me there again this time. Donna Perreault is another dear old friend whose company is essential for losing many an hour in Quarter haunts. Erin Corrigan joined me and helped me blur the lines between day and night. Brett Anderson is always spot on, whether it's food, beer or politics. Cinzia Cavallaro kicked up my efforts a notch through sharp-eyed edits and suggestions.

The 1st edition of this book was written by China Williams.

PHOTOGRAPHER

Ray Laskowitz

Photographer Ray Laskowitz has been taking pictures for almost 30 years in the United States, Asia, and Europe. His imagery is a unique blend of photojournalistic decisive moments and artistic feelings and movement. Shooting New Orleans was a harder assignment than the casual viewer might imagine since Ray lives in New Orleans, not too far from the French Quarter. Like many location photographers, he makes shooting his hometown more complicated then it need be; the city is so remarkable in its culture, food and architecture, it really could photograph itself.

SEND US YOUR FEEDBACK

We love to hear from travellers – your comments keep us on our toes and help make our books better. Our well-travelled team reads every word on what you loved or loathed about this book. Although we cannot reply individually to postal submissions, we always guarantee that your feedback goes straight to the appropriate authors, in time for the next edition – and the most useful submissions are rewarded with a free book. To send us your updates – and find out about Lonely Planet events, newsletters and travel news – visit our award-winning website: 🖳 **www.lonelyplanet.com/feedback.**

Note: We may edit, reproduce and incorporate your comments in Lonely Planet products such as guidebooks, websites and digital products, so let us know if you don't want your comments reproduced or your name acknowledged. For a copy of our privacy policy visit 🖳 www.lonelyplanet.com/privacy.

Introducing New Orleans

New Orleans is a fantasyland, one where enjoying pleasure takes precedence. Where fun is something to be shared and enjoyed. Where marching to your own beat – or someone else's, just as long as there's a beat – is enshrined in the culture. How else to account for a place that pours its heart and soul into an annual spectacle called Mardi Gras?

It's a place where its emblematic sound, jazz, was born in pleasure (the bordellos of a 100 years ago) and where listening to it is always a pleasure. There are clubs and bars to match every taste. And the hours? True fantasy! Some places never close, and you can get your drink to go. And you may want that cup in hand as you explore the city's wilder side, from voodoo haunts to above-ground cemeteries. You're definitely not in Kansas anymore.

New Orleans food is a fantasy of bold flavors and fiery tastes with no compromise to moderation. Eating is a ritual to be savored and beloved restaurants serve meals that can stretch on for large parts of the day. Sated from your food fantasy, ponder over artists' fantasies at the myriad of galleries, or stroll under the Spanish moss-draped oaks arching over the likes of St Charles Avenue like the pillars of a cathedral. For many, the French Quarter is the ultimate fantasy, with its fanciful wrought-iron balconies, clip-clop of horses, tap-tap of street dancers and flicker of gas-lit lamps.

However New Orleans' fantastical attractions does not mean New Orleans is a fairy tale. The civic focus on parties over prosperity means that there's plenty of urban grit, and modern realities dance around its edges. This is no antiseptic playground. It's a real place, unlike anywhere else in the US – or the world – and it's mighty darn fun.

Popular Bourbon St after a few too many drinks

Neighborhoods

New Orleans' major attractions are in the **French Quarter**, which is a compact zone bounded by Canal St, Esplanade Ave, N Rampart St and the river. This is the oldest section with the most foreign influences. It is also the most visited. The architecture here is utterly charming, and music seems to seep from the drain spouts. It's best to get around the Quarter by foot (most French Quarter sights in this book do not list transport options for this reason). You'll easily become trapped within its confines, reluctant to venture beyond Canal St, but do yourself a favor and explore outside the Quarter for the full picture.

Downriver from Esplanade Ave is the **Faubourg Marigny**, which melts imperceptibly into the **Bywater**. The Marigny was the mistress zone where Creole gentlemen would purchase homes for their lovers, typically free women of color. The modest cottages have since been adopted by artists and bohemians, who construct huge art projects in their backyards and live quiet lives of supreme eccentricity. Frenchmen St has become the place to go to at night, with clubs catering to those who eschew the wantonness of Bourbon St.

On the upriver side of Canal St, which historically divided the older charm of the French Quarter from the younger American sector, is the **Central Business District** (CBD). Upriver from Poydras St, the once-derelict **Warehouse District** has sprouted high-quality art galleries and major tourist draws such as the National D-Day Museum and the Ogden Museum of Southern Art.

Once you cross Hwy 90, you've entered the hip **Lower Garden District**, where wealthy Americans showed the austere Creoles how to spend money. The neighborhood has recently been adopted by coffee-drinking, tattooed youngsters and urban revivalists. Upriver from Jackson Ave is the **Garden District**; it replaced the Lower Garden District in the race to build the bigger and better house and was in turn replaced by **Uptown**, upriver from Louisiana Ave. Audubon Park and Zoo, and Tulane University make Uptown an interesting destination on the St Charles streetcar. Beyond Uptown is the modest neighborhood of **Riverbend**, so named for the river's dramatic turn.

Going northwest of the Quarter, you can follow the old oaks and old homes of Esplanade Ave through gentrifying **Esplanade Ridge** and on to **Mid-City**, home to the joys of City Park and Jazz Fest.

Off the Beaten Track

If you hit New Orleans during its peak, the Quarter will be jammed – you will wait for everything from tables to hurricanes. To escape the crowds, rent a bike or hop on a street-car and hightail it to Uptown where the pace is slower. Audubon Park is a regenerated green space, where you can ride the paved trails or climb a live oak. If shopping therapy calms the nerves, cruise the funky shops along Magazine St in the Lower Garden District. The Canal St ferry has plenty of room for sightseers, and offers a glimpse of the wide open spaces of the Mississippi River.

Itineraries

New Orleans' festivals, like Mardi Gras and Jazz Fest, rightfully suck in the masses for their spectacle and frolic, but they can also suck up your time, leaving little to truly explore the city. To get to know the fantasy and the reality, come during the off-season and fill your day with walks, meals, cocktails, plenty of music and, yes, a pause or two on a bench under a huge oak.

For the itineraries described here, just add them together sequentially, depending on the number of days you have

DAY ONE

Start the day with beignets (doughnuts)and café au lait at Café du Monde (p49). Wander Royal and Chartres Sts for an unstructured appreciation of the French Quarter's architecture. For lunch grab a muffuletta at Central Grocery (p50), some raw oysters at Acme Oyster House (p49) or a fried oyster po'boy at Johnny's Po'Boy (p51). Visit some of the historic homes and buildings and walk along the Mississippi River (p15). Make dinner reservations at one of the top Quarter restaurants. Afterwards do some French Quarter barhopping (p62) and imbibe the wee hours with some Bourbon St madness (p12).

DAY TWO

Do brunch at Brennan's New Orleans (p49) to shake off the hangover. Otherwise, a morning tour of the cemeteries or the history of the French Quarter will work up an appetite for an early lunch at Uglesich's (p58). Ride the St Charles streetcar (p36) uptown to the end, or get off in the Garden District (p35) for a stroll. Grab an evening cocktail on the patio at the Columns Hotel (p72) and eat dinner at one of the city's contemporary restaurants. Celebrate late into the night at one of the smokin' music clubs.

Worst of New Orleans
- Swampy summer weather
- Pockets of poverty and crime
- Vast crowds for popular events
- No right-of-way for pedestrians
- Slack-jawed tourists blocking the sidewalk

Swampy summer in Barataria Preserve (p37)

DAY THREE

Visit the National D-Day Museum (p23), Ogden Museum of Southern Art (p24) and the nearby Julia St galleries (p24). Get lunch at an old favorite such as Mother's Restaurant (p55) and go for ride on the Mississippi on the authentic steamboat *Natchez* (p39). Or head out for a shopping spree on Magazine St. Eat like a native at one of the superb neighborhood restaurants then cruise the hip nightclubs of Frenchmen St.

Highlights

MARDI GRAS

Can you let your hair down if it's a wig? Who knows, but during Mardi Gras everyone tries to let it down, get down and keep it down. It's a celebration where the usual good cheer is kicked up not just one notch but 20. From parties in the streets to more reasons to have 'just one more' at every bar in town, Mardi Gras isn't just an event, it's a mood. A time of fun without bounds, when you can wear what you want – or as little as you want – and everybody is your new best friend. Where the looming deadline of Lenten rectitude is met by frenzy.

INFORMATION
Arthur Hardy's Mardi Gras Guide is available for purchase in bookstores each year before Twelfth Night. The *New Orleans Times-Picayune* and *Gambit* also publish their own guides to Mardi Gras, or contact the New Orleans Metropolitan Convention and Visitors Bureau, Inc (☎ 566-5011; 800-672-6124; 🖳 www.neworleans cvb.com). Future Mardi Gras dates are February 28, 2006; February 20, 2007; February 5, 2008.

Hide your hangover with a Mardi Gras mask

This Catholic holiday has bawdy pagan origins. Mardi Gras can be traced to the prespring rituals of the Romans, when class and identity were hidden behind masks, social conventions were flouted and hedonism embraced. It came to be known as *carnevale* (farewell to flesh), referring to the fast that would begin on Ash Wednesday. The theatrical nature of Carnival, with its elaborate baroque costumes, was inherited from 17th-century Venice and its commedia dell'arte. France eventually imported the spectacle to its New World outpost of Nouvelle Orléans.

The modern practice of parading during Mardi Gras didn't evolve until the mid-19th century when an elite group of Americans from the Garden District (called the Mistick Krewe of Comus) publicly launched their torch-lit floats in 1857. Mimicking European royalty, the krewes (clubs that sponsor Mardi Gras parades and events) crowned a king who was disguised by a beard, a beaded crown and regal garb. The king was then paraded on elaborate floats, often thematically decorated. Since that time various krewes have invented traditions that collectively make Mardi Gras one of the world's amazing spectacles and parties.

The krewe of Rex is responsible for the official colors of Mardi Gras: purple for justice, green for faith and gold for power. They named their king the 'King of Mardi Gras' and he continues to be the supreme official of the city during the festival.

The now extinct Twelfth Night Revelers introduced 'throws,' which are trinkets tossed to the crowd as the floats pass by. These keepsakes are highly collectible and often depict the krewe's seal or trademark. Look for the ubiquitous beads as well as decorated plastic drinking cups (both unbreakable and unbeatable), various medallions and a plethora of other items that range from the goofy (small plastic tool belts) to the absurd (bizarre plastic figures). In crowded areas a good throw can set off pandemonium as hordes descend on the booty. Spare your fingers by stepping on items rather than putting your own digits under the feet of others.

The most socially evocative group are the Zulus, an African-American krewe who appeared in 1909. Parodying the royal aspects of the White krewes and the popular minstrel shows of the day, the Zulus wore black faces and pseudotribal grass skirts; they crowned their king with a lard-can crown and a banana-stalk scepter. Today, the Zulus have one of the most prized throws: a painted coconut.

Together, these traditions and a myriad more make Mardi Gras unforgettable, unmissable and unsurpassable.

> **DON'T MISS**
> - Wearing a costume, dancing in the streets
> - Endymion, with the biggest float in New Orleans, parading Saturday night
> - Orpheus, with a cast of celebrities, parading Monday night
> - The Zulu parade on Mardi Gras morning in Uptown
> - The Rex float with the *boeuf gras* (fatted cow) float on Mardi Gras morning

Experiencing Carnival

The Carnival season begins on January 6 (Twelfth Night) and runs until Mardi Gras (Fat Tuesday), which varies every year. A small St Charles Ave parade and low-key balls, some open to the public, start the season with a slow methodical rhythm. A bawdy foot parade travels through the French Quarter three Saturdays before Mardi Gras begins. The real parade season starts 12 days before Fat Tuesday, and some of the best fun can be had on the first weekend when everything is more local, more intimate and more accessible. On Lundi Gras (the day before Mardi Gras), the keys to the city are ceremoniously turned over by the mayor to the King of Rex. The major parade routes are the **Uptown Route** (3; St Charles Ave from Napoleon Ave to Canal St) and the **Mid-City Route** (4; City Park down Orleans Ave to Carrollton Ave to Canal St). The grandstands (with paid admission) are set up in front of Gallier Hall in the CBD. Although visitors can't gain access to the society balls where the older krewes crown their kings and queens, modern krewes throw parties that are open to the public. For tickets, call **Orpheus** (☎ 822-7211), **Tucks** (☎ 288-2481) or the gay krewe **Petronius** (☎ 525-4498). And remember, at midnight on Mardi Gras, the cops roll up the streets and roll out the revelers so that everyone has an Ash Wednesday rest, whether they want it or not.

JAZZ & HERITAGE FESTIVAL (4, C4)

In the city credited with inventing jazz, this festival celebrates music and good times like no other. The voices and instruments that are stuffed into clubs all year get to meet the glorious summer sun. More than 12 stages host jazz, zydeco, R&B, bluegrass, gospel and rock.

Stalls run by local restaurants dish up some of the city's famous cuisine, from po'boys and boiled crawfish to gumbo and fried chicken. Local artists and craftspeople also set up shop along the perimeter. The mood is nearly orgasmic at times with impromptu processions from tent to tent.

INFORMATION

- 🖥 www.nojazzfest.com
- ✉ 1751 Gentilly Blvd
- 💲 $20 in advance or $25 at the gate
- 🕐 11am-7pm, last weekend in Apr–first weekend in May
- ⓘ New Orleans Jazz & Heritage Festival (1205 N Rampart St, New Orleans, LA 70116; ☎ 522-4786); buy tickets from Ticketmaster (☎ 522-5555)
- 🚋 City Park streetcar
- 🚌 shuttle from downtown $10 round trip or No 48 Esplanade bus
- 🅿 limited parking $20
- ♿ information line ☎ 558-7849

DON'T MISS

- Gospel tent
- Choosing from nearly 30 crawfish dishes
- Choosing from 12 bands playing at once
- Jazz Fest posters

The Jimmy Thibodeaux Band cranks it up

The heritage part of the 10-day festival is really the main event. It is held over two weekends, beginning each Friday, and fills the Fair Grounds near City Park. Each evening, during all 10 days, you can catch major acts such as Dave Brubeck and BB King at venues around town. Tickets for these events are sold separately from Heritage Fest day passes.

It's hard to imagine not being swept up in the joy of Jazz Fest, especially with acts like Buckwheat Zydeco, Branford Marsalis, Etta James, Santana and Clarence 'Gatemouth' Brown playing.

Jazz Fest draws over 500,000 people and requires advance planning, especially when you're making hotel reservations. Prepare for tropical temperatures: drink lots of water and stand in the shade. Bring a blanket to sit on, some extra toilet paper and a rain poncho. Expecting long lines will let you get into the spirit of things so you can enjoy one grand musical party.

FRENCH QUARTER (6)

The oldest sector of New Orleans, the French Quarter, is by far the most charming and historical. This fascinating area alone is reason for a journey. Visitors come to wander the compact streets and enjoy the architecture. Almost every home has a bricked courtyard or patio, decorated with a fountain and tropical banana trees, ginger plants or palms. The aged beauty of the Quarter truly emerges just after a thunderstorm, when streaks of gold, peach and violet reflect off the ornate cast-iron balconies, where hanging ferns grow more verdant in the saturated light.

INFORMATION

- bound by Esplanade Ave, N Rampart St, Canal St & the river
- ℹ New Orleans Welcome Center (D4; ☎ 566-5031; 529 St Ann St; 9am-5pm)
- 🚍 sidewalks can be crowded
- 🍴 see p49

The Quarter (also known as the Vieux Carré) was laid out in a gridlike pattern in 1721 by French engineers. Many of the original inhabitants were Creole plantation owners who would winter in the city. They would arrive in time for midnight mass at St Louis Cathedral on Christmas Eve and stay through the Mardi Gras season, returning to their Mississippi River plantations on Ash Wednesday.

By the early 20th century, the French Quarter had fallen into disrepair and was scheduled to be razed before preservation efforts of the 1930s saved the district. Restoration of the old houses was so successful that today the Quarter is very much in demand as an address. It's not uncommon for a home that seems entirely unassuming to passersby to sell for more than $1 million.

The area is best explored on foot. Visitors should stray from the well-traveled Bourbon St and Jackson Sq quadrant. Away from the hubbub, the Quarter's inherent charms are easily assimilated. Wander Burgundy St at dusk and neighbors will greet you as one of their own.

Open-Air Markets

Everything from a palate-numbing array of hot sauces to profane T-shirts to oddball strings of beads can be purchased at the **French Market** (E4; ⊠ Decatur St, from St Ann St to Barracks St; ☻ 9am-5pm), whose history dates back more than 200 years. And yes, there's even a small **farmer's market** where you can buy produce.

French fashion in the French Quarter

BOURBON ST (6, C5)

You can get everything on Bourbon St – booze, strippers, music, food. You might go here out of curiosity but you'll soon be sucked into the most raucous open-air adult carnival in the USA. Here it's Mardi Gras at its most shameless, 24/7.

Neon lights blaze with silent intensity, and the steady flow of human traffic squeezes out the cars. The bars blare rock cover tunes and a crowd has assembled around a balcony where Mardi Gras beads are being dispensed in exchange for a flash of some flesh.

INFORMATION

- ⊠ bound by Canal St & Esplanade Ave, btwn Dauphine & Royal Sts
- ☯ 8 blocks are closed to motor vehicles after dark; bar times vary, many are open 24hr
- ♿ sidewalks can be crowded
- ✗ Galatoire's (p50), Clover Grill (p50)

The wholesome-looking housewife is usually the first to take the bait, brazenly lifting her top to deafening cheers. Bourbon St unloosens people at the seams. Next thing you know you've wandered into a techno-thumping, harshly lit booze joint, waffling between sips of hurricanes and grenades. You join the crowd, swept up in the party atmosphere. You might run from one end of the street to the other before venturing into one of the packed clubs, where waiters hawk test tubes of fluorescent-colored liquor and sweaty bodies bump into each other.

You don't need a guide to Bourbon St. It is self-explanatory: go with cash and spend it on whatever you want. Have a good time. Get drunk, yell, vomit, dance, slobber on your friend, stay up till dawn. Everything goes here and it goes every night, all night.

Laissez rouler les bons temps (let the good times roll).

Above the Crowd

The balconies overlooking Bourbon St are prime party real estate all year. Here you can ponder the drunken masses below while bartering beads for glimpses of flesh. Some balconies are part of hotels, where noon is the hour of sleep; others are part of bars, where your stairway to hell lies just inside the door. Two of the wildest are **Tropical Isle** (6, C4; ☎ 529-4109; 721 Bourbon St) and **Bourbon St Blues Company** (6, C5; ☎ 566-1507; 441 Bourbon St).

Bourbon St neon – everywhere, anytime

NEW ORLEANS JAZZ

Jazz is the heartbeat of New Orleans. No city has a sound so closely connected to it. New Orleans is a musical melting pot where Whites and Blacks trade their cultural heritage – a place where European instruments meet African syncopation and invention. From the tourist dives on Bourbon St to gritty clubs in every neighborhood, the jazz here is loud, live, brassy and sassy.

In New Orleans, European operas and Congo Sq's African dances joined the city's celebration of music. Homespun tunes burst forth from the bordellos of Storyville, and were soon heard from the classy joints of Uptown to the dives of Bywater. Local cornetist Buddy Bolden (1877–1931) was the 'King of Jazz.' Stories recount that Bolden once played his cornet so loudly that it actually exploded. His style influenced leagues of younger musicians, including pianist Jelly Roll Morton (1890–1941).

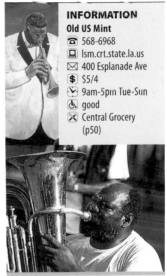

> **INFORMATION**
> **Old US Mint**
> ☎ 568-6968
> ▯ lsm.crt.state.la.us
> ✉ 400 Esplanade Ave
> 💲 $5/4
> 🕐 9am-5pm Tue-Sun
> ♿ good
> ✖ Central Grocery (p50)

New Orleans' most famous musician, Louis 'Satchmo' Armstrong (1901–71), came of age during the 1920s. He gave jazz a swing that was so frequently mimicked that

Big, bad and brassy

his music seems conventional today. Other stars who achieved fame include soprano saxophonist Sidney Bechet, clarinetist Barney Bigard and trumpeter Louis Prima.

The jazz exhibit at the **Old US Mint** (6, E4) recounts this history with displays of sheet music, instruments, soundtracks and artists' biographies. Even lukewarm jazz enthusiasts will be intrigued by the candid shots of New Orleans musicians and jazz funerals.

Jazz Anywhere

WWOZ (90.7 FM) is New Orleans' beloved volunteer-run station that plays jazz in all its forms, plus the many other styles of music dear to the ears of locals. Get in the mood for your trip by listening to its eclectic sound live over the Internet (www.wwoz.org).

Aficionados should definitely visit the **Hogan Jazz Archives** (3, C2; ☎ 865-5688; 3rd fl, Jones Hall, Tulane University; 🕐 9am-4:45pm). The National Park Service's **New Orleans Jazz National Historical Park** (6, E4; ☎ 589-4841; 916 N Peters St; 🕐 9am-5pm Tue-Sat) has musical heritage displays and live performances.

JACKSON SQUARE (6, D4-5)

With a front-row view of the Mississippi River, Jackson Sq and its surrounding buildings were the city's nerve center during the colonial period. Originally named Place d'Armes, the square was rededicated to the hero of the Battle of New Orleans, Andrew Jackson, in 1856 with a snapshotlike sculpture of the general tipping his hat in adieu, astride his rearing horse.

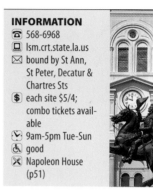

INFORMATION
- ☎ 568-6968
- 🖥 lsm.crt.state.la.us
- ✉ bound by St Ann, St Peter, Decatur & Chartres Sts
- 💲 each site $5/4; combo tickets available
- 🕐 9am-5pm Tue-Sun
- ♿ good
- 🍴 Napoleon House (p51)

Facing the square, the triple-spired **St Louis Cathedral** was the spiritual focal point for the Creole populace. Dedicated to Louis IX, France's sainted king, the church was completed in 1794, with significant remodeling in 1851. The interior of the church is renaissance and baroque, with many ornate murals and side chapels.

If facing the cathedral, to your left is the **Cabildo** (p22), the former meeting house of the Spanish and French governments. The Louisiana Purchase was signed here. Now it houses a museum on Louisiana and New Orleans history.

The Cabildo's twin, on the other side of the cathedral, is the **Presbytère** (p24), which served many purposes during the colonial period. It is now home to the Louisiana State Museum's Mardi Gras exhibit.

Facing each other from across the square are the block-long **Pontalba Apartments**, constructed in 1850 by Madame Micaëla Pontalba. She was the daughter of Don Andrés Almonester y Roxas, the Spanish benefactor who funded the rebuilding of the Cabildo, Presbytère and cathedral after the citywide fires. Her story is more interesting than her legacy of row houses. She grew up in a powerful New Orleans family and was joined to another prominent family through marriage. The couple moved to Paris, where the husband's family attempted to procure her fortune; she resisted and eventually separated from her husband. Frustrated, the father-in-law shot her and then turned the gun on himself. Madame Pontalba recovered from the wounds and returned to New Orleans in 1844. She refurbished the buildings on Jackson Sq, adding the arcaded row houses bearing her name. The **1850 House Museum** (p25) has a self-guided tour through a period-decorated apartment in the Lower Pontalba building.

DON'T MISS
- Free tour of St Louis Cathedral
- Watching the artists and palm-readers vie for space in the square
- View of Jackson Sq from Moonwalk Park (p28)

MISSISSIPPI RIVER

The 'father of waters' is a determined yet meandering artery that's seen more of the USA than most of the country's citizens. Waking up in Minnesota, the river encourages other watercourses to join it on its 2400-mile trip south; through its powers of persuasion, it ultimately drains 41% of the USA. At a particularly dramatic bend, only 160 miles from the Gulf of Mexico, New Orleans built its livelihood off this workhorse.

INFORMATION
- ⊠ foot of the French Quarter
- ☾ dusk is the prettiest time
- ✗ Café du Monde (p49)

At first, river travel was slow; the river didn't become a viable highway until the advent of the steamboat in 1807. In 1812 the *New Orleans* was launched at a speed of 3mph from Pittsburgh, Pennsylvania. A remarkably short three months later, it was the first steam powered vessel to reach New Orleans. Within a decade, the city's population mushroomed as a result of river traffic.

The river changes its course like a dancing boxer dodging an anticipated punch. Coaxing the river onto a more reliable path has occupied engineers since 1735, when a 3ft high levee system was built 30 miles upstream and 12 miles downstream. The river jumped its banks in the spring of 1927, resulting in government-funded higher levee walls, and later an 8½-mile above-ground flood wall around New Orleans. A total of 22 pumping stations keep New Orleans from filling up like a basin, and every spring, inhabitants watch the river nervously as it silently swells with snowmelt.

DON'T MISS
- A ride on the Canal St ferry (p30)
- A *Natchez* steamboat river cruise (p39)
- A picnic on a waterside bench
- A stroll from Moonwalk Park to Riverwalk (p28)

See the light by cruising the Mississippi

On mild days there are numerous sunny benches along the river in the French Quarter where you can sip a refreshment, munch some sustenance and watch the parade of barges, cargo ships and tourist boats go by. The river is a whopping 200ft deep at this point: don't emulate numerous doomed and drunken tourists who have jumped in for a swim.

NEW ORLEANS CUISINE

An attraction in itself, New Orleans cuisine is called Creole, and to describe its origins is to recount the city's history. In the beginning there was French food, characterized by rich sauces and pureed soups, constructed from a base called roux (flour browned with fat) and *mirepoix* (sautéed celery, onions and carrots). The Spanish came along and swapped bell peppers for carrots, which didn't like the Louisiana heat. Seasonings from the New World forests, such as bay leaves, cayenne pepper and filé (ground sassafras), were added by Native Americans.

INFORMATION

- ⏱ many restaurants outside the French Quarter are closed Sun
- 🖥 The *New Orleans Times-Picayune* (www.nola.com) is an excellent source for restaurant reviews and news
- ⓘ see p29 for information on local cooking schools

Breakfast at the Bluebird Café (p56)

The miniature lobster, known locally as crawfish, and other fruits of the sea were also directed into the pot from Native American fishing holes. The Africans who commanded the kitchens introduced the method of slow cooking and deep frying. Okra, an African refugee, also joined the mélange as a thickening agent. These ingredients are the beginnings of some of New Orleans' most famous exports – jambalaya, red beans and rice, and gumbo.

The cuisine's staples speak of a boundless harvest, where forests and waters provide seasonal variety. Seafood, including shrimp, oyster and crawfish, are handled in countless ways: they are sautéed in butter, deep-fried in cornmeal batter, or boiled with copious amounts of spices. You will be able to enjoy this feast for the palate throughout the city, in restaurants both humble and grand. Come thin.

Creole versus Cajun

In the watery Louisiana backwoods, French exiles from Nova Scotia put ingredients such as seafood and game over the fire to boil. Their cuisine (and culture) came to be called Cajun, and reflected ethnic influences similar to those of Cajun's cosmopolitan cousin, Creole. Cajun cooking, however, is simpler and further removed from traditional French cuisine. Andouille gumbo and crawfish étouffée might appear at both Cajun and Creole tables, while *boudin* (black sausage) and cracklins (deep-fried pork skin) are Creole comfort food.

WAREHOUSE DISTRICT (5)

Warehouses for galleries and lofts for artists are just some of the attractions of the ever-growing Warehouse District. Just south of the CBD, the area is defined by blocks of sturdy 19th-century brick buildings. Many hotels – often in heavily remodeled historic buildings – are located here and serve the Convention Center by the river.

Strolling these streets yields many surprises. There are galleries galore with local and international artists on display along **Julia St** (p24). Several of the city's best cultural institutions are here as well. The **Ogden Museum of Southern Art** (p24) is in a beautiful building that opened in 2004. Its captivating collection is an essential stop before venturing out to the galleries. Another top spot is **Louisiana ArtWorks** (p23), a center for both working artists and visitors.

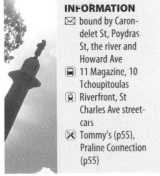

INFORMATION
- ✉ bound by Carondelet St, Poydras St, the river and Howard Ave
- 🚌 11 Magazine, 10 Tchoupitoulas
- 🚋 Riverfront, St Charles Ave streetcars
- 🍴 Tommy's (p55), Praline Connection (p55)

A real highlight is the **National D-Day Museum** (p23), which was the dream of the late historian and author Stephen Ambrose. With help from celebrities, including the *Saving Private Ryan* duo of Tom Hanks and Steven Spielberg, the museum breaks the mold of war museums with its focus on the human cost of war. Few will fail to be moved by the personal stories of the invasion of Europe.

War Stories
The popularity of the National D-Day Museum (p23) has led to a plan to dramatically enlarge the facility and rename it America's National WWII Museum. The $150 million project will cover several blocks of the Warehouse District and will be completed in phases through 2009.

Count the cost of war at the D-Day Museum

The district is home to what is arguably the city's most famous restaurant, **Emeril's** (p54). The lofty converted warehouse space booms with the eponymous owner's trademark energy. Other restaurants have opened nearby, and the entire area enjoys a great reputation for dining. Late at night, **Howlin' Wolf** (p65) rocks with progressive, jazz and blues sounds.

Although there's nary a cast-iron balcony in sight, the Warehouse District is an essential part of any visit to the Crescent City. Where the French Quarter may seem wonderfully frozen in time, this place builds on the old with some of the best of new New Orleans.

CITY PARK   (4, B2-4)

The proud live oaks draped in Spanish moss, combined with the first-rate museum, theme parks and botanical garden, make City Park a well-rounded family destination (see also p33). With the completion of the streetcar line to the park, it is more accessible for visitors than ever, and makes for a good half-day adventure.

Founded in 1910, **New Orleans Museum of Art** (4, B4; p24) shows a good range of art that includes works by one-time New Orleans resident Edgar Degas. Recently the big news here concerns not the works inside but rather the works outside, where the news is truly big. The new **Sculpture Garden** (4, B4) shows 50 works in a spacious setting around a lagoon. Of special note are works by Henry Moore and Fernando Botero. Like much of the rest of the park, the grounds are dappled with sun filtering through the 150-year-old oak trees.

INFORMATION

- ☎ 482-4888
- 🖳 www.neworleans citypark.com
- ✉ cnr Esplanade Ave & Wisner Blvd
- 💲 botanical garden $5/2
- 🕐 park dawn-dusk; botanical garden 10am-4:30pm Tue-Sun
- 🚌 48 Esplanade
- 🚋 City Park streetcar
- ♿ good
- 🍴 Museum Courtyard Cafe, Café Degas (p59)

The **Botanical Garden** (4, B4) offers a 12-acre course on Louisiana flora. Designed and built by the federal works project, the garden features a unique art deco pond surrounded by bricked paths, a rose garden and a butterfly garden.

Many swords and pistols have been drawn at the somber **Dueling Oaks** (4, B4), of which only one original tree remains. One famous duel involved the master fencer Gilbert Rosiere. The opera and the theater frequently moved Gilbert to tears, and on one occasion, a man laughed at this display. The offended Gilbert threw his glove, indicating a challenge to a duel. The sensitive Gilbert spared the man's life but left him with a disfiguring scar, a reminder to laugh only at people who aren't fencers.

Examine art, or your feet, in City Park

Live Oaks

Pick up the free oak trees walking-tour brochure at any of the City Park attractions. Among the highlights is the McDonogh Oak, the park's oldest at over 600 years of age. This veteran is 72ft tall and shades a radius of 153ft.

AUDUBON INSTITUTE

Whether you get around on two, four, six or eight legs, or by flipping your fin or flapping your wings, the Audubon Institute has your number.

A great cultural institution, the organization is dedicated to preserving nature and wildlife. It operates numerous facilities and attractions, and is based at **Audubon Park** (p28) in Uptown. Its main event is the world-renowned **Audubon Zoo** (p32), which has everything from white tigers to orangutans, all featured in fascinating enclosures. The **Louisiana Swamp** shows how Cajuns lived off the land and water, and who in the animal kingdom they lived with.

Right on the river, off the French Quarter, the **Audubon Aquarium of the Americas** (p32) is the other big tuna in the Audubon ferment. It features thousands of fish and a very cool glass tunnel that lets you walk through the middle of a huge tank. There is also a nearby **Entergy IMAX Theater** (p67).

Third in the Audubon sphere is the **Audubon Louisiana Nature Center**, perhaps the most sublime attraction. Sprawling over 80 acres in eastern New Orleans, there is a small museum to whet the appetite for the real fun, which lies along the mile-long boardwalk through the swamp. Here you can see all manner of Louisiana natives, such as nutrias, alligators and birds. Another feature of the center is the animal recovery area where sick and injured animals are brought for rehabilitation. This is a good way to see critters which might otherwise be hard to spot up close. If you'd rather gaze at something far away, there's an on-site planetarium.

INFORMATION

Audubon Louisiana Nature Center

☎ 246-5672

🖳 www.audubon institute.org

✉ 5601 Read Blvd

💲 $5/3, combination packages available

🕙 9am-5pm Tue-Fri, 10am-5pm Sat, noon-5pm Sun

🚖 cab or drive

🅿 free

♿ good

Audubon Zoo – Froot Loops anyone?

Gorillas by Boat

One of the fun features of the Audubon Institute's Zoo and Aquarium of the Americas is that you can take a boat (☎ 586-8777; $17/8.50; 🕙 hourly 10am-5pm) between the two riverside attractions. Several times a day the boat makes the circuit along the Mississippi River, providing a glimpse of the waters where other tourist boats don't venture. You could take the boat one way and then combine a park stroll with a ride on the St Charles streetcar.

CEMETERIES

New Orleans' love of tradition is most easily demonstrated in its famous cemeteries. These small cities of the dead are traversed by narrow paths between rows of boxlike tombs just tall enough to form a maze. Some are pristinely whitewashed, with ornamental roofs; others have bowed to time, their facades exposing bare brick and wild grasses have sprouted from the joints.

Most tombs are aboveground, reflecting Spanish burial tradition. The communal tombs are inherited by the next generation. The interred bodies aren't embalmed and the oven-shaped vaults reach decomposing temperatures. This leaves room for the next inhabitant to be laid to rest a year and a day after the previous burial.

Of the cemeteries in New Orleans, **St Louis Cemetery No 1** (6, B4) is the oldest (1789), with tombs outdating most buildings in the French Quarter. This decaying boneyard houses voodoo priestess Marie Laveau and Bernard de Marigny (whose plantation was divided up to build Faubourg Marigny). The acid trip in *Easy Rider* was filmed here. This cemetery is not safe to wander in alone; joining a tour not only increases safety, it adds to your enjoyment of the cemetery's history.

Situated in the Garden District, **Lafayette Cemetery No 1** (3, G4) contains several tombs that bear Irish and German names, many of the people buried here were killed by the yellow fever epidemics.

INFORMATION

- ⊠ St Louis Cemetery No 1 (cnr Basin & Conti Sts); Lafayette Cemetery No 1 (Washington Ave, btwn Prytania & Coliseum Sts)
- $ free
- ☺ St Louis 9am-4pm; Lafayette 9am-2:30pm
- ⓘ tours of St Louis by Historic New Orleans (☎ 947-2120); tours of Lafayette by Save Our Cemeteries, Inc (☎ 525-3377)
- 🚋 Lafayette Cemetery No 1: St Charles streetcar to Washington Ave
- 🚌 St Louis Cemetery No 1: go with a tour group

DON'T MISS

- Marie Laveau's tomb and the Italian Mutual Benevolent Society tomb in St Louis No 1
- Jefferson Fire Company No 22 crypt at Lafayette
- Tours by Save Our Cemeteries, Inc (p39)

NEW ORLEANS STREETCARS

New Orleans now operates three streetcar lines. This growing network is both a great way for visitors to get around and an attraction in itself.

Everyone's favorite is also the oldest. Like an olive-green caterpillar, steered by its alert antennae, the **St Charles streetcar** plots a straight path through the canopied oaks and grassy neutral ground of the Garden District and Uptown. It's a lovely ride, which can be taken to a specific destination or just for the ramble. Seat yourself on a mahogany bench beside the huge open windows, eavesdrop on your gossiping neighbors, and hold tight as you're pitched forward with a sudden stop to pick up commuters or tourists. Detestable Ignatius J Reilly from Confederacy of Dunces rode this route from his Irish Channel home to his hot-dog vending job in the French Quarter.

Since 1835, many people have ridden to and fro on this line, which started out as a horse-drawn vehicle called the *New Orleans & Carrollton Railroad*. In 1893 the horse was replaced with electricity, which is still used today. It is the oldest continuously operating line in the country.

In 2004, the St Charles line got a companion in a much-heralded network expansion that saw two new lines push up from the French Quarter along **Canal St** to **Metairie Cemetery** and **City Park**. These air-conditioned streetcars are designed to look old. Service is frequent and ridership is already exceeding forecasts.

A third streetcar line, the **Riverfront**, links the French Quarter with the Convention Center using non-air-conditioned cars.

INFORMATION
- ☎ 248-3900
- 🖥 www.norta.com
- $ $1 25
- 🕐 every 6-16min during peak hours, less frequently at other times; St Charles and Cemeteries lines 24hr
- ♿ information line 827-7433

Watch the world blur by from a streetcar

DON'T MISS
- Riding the City Park line all the way from Esplanade Ave in the Quarter
- St Charles streetcar tour (p36)
- Getting a window seat

Sights & Activities

MUSEUMS & GALLERIES

New Orleans museums are as eclectic as the city; galleries reflect the plethora of local artistic talent.

Amistad Research Center (3, C3) The *Amistad* was a small, Cuba-bound schooner illegally transporting Africans to enslavement in 1839. After a mutiny, the schooner was misdirected to New York, where the Africans were jailed. Named in the boat's honor, this is one of the country's largest repositories of African-American historical materials, including 250,000 photos.
☎ 865-5535 ⌨ www.amistadresearchcenter.org ✉ Tilton Hall, Tulane University 💲 free ⌚ 9am-4pm Mon-Sat 🚋 St Charles at Audubon Park

Backstreet Cultural Museum (6, C3) 'Backstreet' refers literally to the streets in the African-American community outside the surveillance of White authority. It was here that jazz and second-line parades of masked Mardi Gras Indians took over the usual street activities. In an old funeral home in Tremé, Sylvester Francis runs tours of his collection of New Orleans African-American memorabilia.
☎ 522-4806 ⌨ www.backstreetcultural museum.com ✉ 1116 St Claude Ave 💲 $5 ⌚ 10am-5pm Tue-Sat 🚗 cab or drive

Cabildo (6, D4) This scattershot collection, belonging to the Louisiana State Museum, displays artifacts from the city's colonial history with digressions on how Creoles amused themselves. The centerpiece of the museum is the bronze death mask of Napoleon, presented to the city by the emperor's bedside doctor. A lock of Andrew Jackson's hair, an iron collar, and other odds and ends push the visitor through the Battle of New Orleans to Mississippi River trade and modern times.
☎ 568-6968 ⌨ lsm.crt.state.la.us ✉ Jackson Sq 💲 $5/free ⌚ 9am-5pm Tue-Sat 🚻 good

Confederate Museum (5, D5) Claiming to be the oldest museum in the state, this Civil War museum displays swords, flags and Jefferson Davis memorabilia. Other items crammed into waist-high display cases include personal effects from common soldiers, and pieces of Robert E Lee's silver service. The exhibits aren't particularly professional, but building buffs will be intrigued by the Confederate Memorial Hall's terra-cotta arches and interior exposed cypress beams.
☎ 523-4522 ⌨ www.confederatemuseum.com ✉ 929 Camp St 💲 $5/2 ⌚ 10am-4pm Mon-Sat 🚋 St Charles at Lee Circle

Contemporary Arts Center (5, D5) CAC runs dozens of changing exhibits spotlighting Louisiana artists working in a variety of media. The center's performance space hosts dance and music events, and an education division offers workshops for children. There is a small Internet café.
☎ 528-3805 ⌨ www.cacno.org ✉ 900 Camp St 💲 $5/3 ⌚ 11am-5pm Tue-Sun 🚋 St Charles at Lee Circle 🚻 good 🚻

Another brick in the floor at the National D-Day Museum

Historic New Orleans Collection (6, C5)

For a fantastic history lesson, visit the galleries of this non-profit organization staffed by longtime residents. Guides lead groups through materials such as Iberville's request to establish a colony and Louisiana Purchase documents. Tours of the benefactors' renovated town house are also given. The 1st-floor exhibit space is air-conditioned, free and has good changing exhibits.
☎ 598-7171 💻 www .hnoc.org ✉ 533 Royal St 💲 $5 🕐 10am-4:30pm Tue-Sat 🚾 good

Louisiana ArtWorks (5, D5)

Set to open in 2005, this huge building covers two city blocks. Promising to add yet more vibrancy to the city's thriving arts scene, ArtWorks will provide studio space and support to scores of local artists. Uniquely, it will also have a large visitor component, which promises to allow for a fascinating cross-pollination.
☎ 523-1465 ✉ 725 Howard Ave 💲 $7/5 🕐 10am-5pm Tue-Sat, noon-5pm Sun 🚋 St Charles at Lee Circle 🚾 good

Jean Lafitte National Historic Park & Preserve

The National Park Service (NPS) French Quarter Visitor Center (6, D5) is the place to get information for this far-flung and six-site national park. Offering changing exhibits on local culture and history, as well as popular walking tours, the center is also the place to get information on the Chalmette Battlefield (2, F3) east of town. There Major General Andrew Jackson defeated a superior British force to ensure that the United States kept control of the former French lands that formed the Louisiana Purchase.
☎ 589-2636 💻 www .nps.gov/jcla/jelaweb .htm ✉ 419 Decatur St 💲 free 🕐 9am-5pm 🚾 good

National D-Day Museum (5, D5)

This museum is a top-notch, Smithsonian-quality experience. The upper floors trace the history of WWII, using personal stories. Much attention is focused on the heroism, sacrifice and waste of the fateful invasion of the European continent, as well as other campaigns. The 1st floor honors Higgins Industries, the New Orleans–based boat builder contracted to develop amphibious landing vehicles. Modified versions of crafts used by trappers and the oil industry, Higgins' shallow draft boats were used to storm the beaches at Normandy.
☎ 527-6012 💻 www .ddaymuseum.org ✉ 945 Magazine St 💲 $10/5 🕐 9am-5pm 🚋 St Charles at Lee Circle 🚾 good

Newcomb Art Gallery/ Woldenberg Art Center (3, C2)

Newcomb College was founded in 1886 to provide women with a liberal arts education. It soon became famous for its Arts and Crafts–style pottery, which was influenced by the English Arts and Crafts movement. Female students weren't allowed to throw their own pots and many famous male potters, including George Orr, were employed for the dirty work. Traveling exhibits and student artwork can be viewed at the gallery

Art at the Cabildo

☎ 865-5328 💻 www .newcomb.tulane.edu ✉ cnr Broadway & Willow Sts, Tulane campus 💲 free 🕐 10am-5pm Mon-Fri, noon-5pm Sat & Sun 🚋 St Charles at Broadway 🚾 good

New Orleans African-American Museum (6, C2)

In a fine 1829 Creole villa, this small museum exhibits traveling shows of African-American art. Displays have included everything from Martin Luther King Jr in New Orleans, to artworks by schoolchildren. The museum is in the Tremé, a neighborhood where free people of color owned property prior to the Civil War.
☎ 529-2976 💻 www .noaam.org ✉ 1418 Governor Nicholls St 💲 $5/2 🕐 10am-5pm Mon-Fri, 10am-2pm Sat 🚗 cab or drive

Julia St Galleries (5, E4)

The top collection of galleries in New Orleans can be found along Julia St in the Warehouse District. In a harmonious blend with the nearby Ogden Museum of Southern Art (below), Contemporary Arts Center (p67) and Louisiana ArtWorks (p23), the galleries offer works by international and local artists. And don't just stick to Julia St, the surrounding streets have a few good ones as well.

New Orleans Center for the Photographic Arts (3, J4)

A center with darkrooms and other facilities for both hobbyists and artists, there are also regular exhibitions of works by local photographers. Travel is a recurring theme.
☎ 522-3211 💻 www.neworleansdarkroom.com ✉ 1927 Sophie Wright Pl $ free 🕑 10am-7pm Sat-Tue & Thu, 10am-9pm Fri 🚌 11 Magazine at Sophie Wright Pl ♿ fair

New Orleans Museum of Art (4, B4)

The city's main gallery has an eclectic collection that includes major works by European and American masters. Besides a good smattering of works completed since the 17th century (including a Degas painted in New Orleans), there is a floor of Asian, African and Pre-Columbian art. The photographic section has some very choice works. There's a small café.
☎ 488-2631 💻 www.noma.org ✉ 1 Collins Diboll Circle, City Park $ $8/4 🕑 10am-5pm Tue, Wed, Fri-Sun, 10am-8:30pm Thu 🚌 City Park ♿ good

Ogden Museum of Southern Art (5, D5)

The Ogden Museum is a premier showcase of Southern art. Through folk art, modern painting, traditional crafts and poignant photography, the South speaks fluently about itself and its struggles. A fabulous new five-storey building opened in 2004, helping to make this a must-see for art lovers. The captions are superb, providing both context and background. An exhibit on Mardi Gras in 1925 is captivating. A top-floor patio overlooks the Warehouse District.
☎ 539-9600 💻 www.ogdenmuseum.org ✉ 925 Camp St $ $10/5 🕑 9:30am-5:30pm Tue, Wed, Fri-Sun, 9:30am-8:30pm Thu 🚌 St Charles at Lee Circle ♿ good

Presbytère (6, D4)

The 'Mardi Gras: It's Carnival Time in Louisiana' exhibit at the 1813 Presbytère is a must-see for Fat Tuesday regulars and novices. Elaborate costumes, video footage and piped music create a dynamic carnival energy, even within the sterile halls of a state museum. Crown jewels from the old-line krewes, famous throws and doubloons, and climb-aboard floats attempt to catalog the immense cultural history of this homegrown festival.
☎ 568-6968 💻 lsm.crt.state.la.us ✉ Jackson Sq $ $5/4 🕑 9am-5pm Tue-Sun ♿ good

Street Pronunciation Guide

To pronounce the mutt of Spanish, French and English street names requires some linguistic acrobatics. Seemingly French words are anglicized, English words are gallicized and other words require a local knowledge. Here are few to cut your teeth on:
- Burgundy (bur-*gun*-dee)
- Chartres (*chart*-ers)
- Conti (cont-*eye*)
- Esplanade (es-plan-*aid*)
- Tchoupitoulas (chop-uh-*too*-lus)
- Carondelet (car-ahn-dah-*lette*)

HISTORIC HOMES & NOTABLE ARCHITECTURE

Beauregard-Keyes House Museum (6, D4)

General PGT Beauregard, commander of the Civil War's first shots, lived in this 1826 Greek Revival house for only 18 months. The longer resident was Francis Parkinson Keyes, author of more than 51 novels, including *Dinner at Antoine's* (1948). Period pieces decorate the house, while Keyes' doll and ceramic collections occupy the back cottage. Note the unusual twin staircases out front.

☎ 523-7257 ✉ 1113 Chartres St $ $5/2 ☾ 10am-3pm Mon-Sat, tours on the hr

Degas House (4, C5)

The Impressionist painter Edgar Degas came to New Orleans for four months in 1872 to visit his Creole cousins. During his visit he completed 18 paintings and four sketches, the most famous of which is *A Cotton Office in New Orleans*. The tour introduces visitors to the period and the family members portrayed in the painter's New Orleans paintings. You can also book a B&B room here.

☎ 821-5009 ☐ www .degashouse.com ✉ 2306 Esplanade Ave $ $10/5 ☾ by appointment; 1hr tour ☐ 48 Esplanade at N Tonti St

1850 House Museum (6, D4)

In the lower Pontalba Building, this row house, with its detailed ironwork, replicates how a middle-class family might have lived. The self-guided tour views the period-decorated rooms, many no bigger than your closet-sized hotel room. Visit this house in conjunction with visits to other parts of the Louisiana State Museum.

☎ 568-6968 ☐ lsm.crt .state.la.us ✉ 523 St Ann St $ $5/4 ☾ 9am-5pm Tue-Sun

Faulkner House (6, D4)

In 1925 the French Quarter was a slum, discarded by the wealthy and adopted by poor immigrants. That year William Faulkner rented an apartment overlooking the garden behind St Louis Cathedral. While living in the city he described as a 'courtesan, not old and yet no longer young,' Faulkner worked for the *Times-Picayune* and published his first novel, *Soldier's Pay* (1926). Faulkner's room is now one of the city's finest bookstores (p46).

☎ 586-1609 ✉ 624 Pirate's Alley $ by donation ☾ by appointment

Gallier House Museum (6, D4)

Many of New Orleans' Greek Revival buildings were designed by James Gallier Sr and James Gallier Jr. The son built this technologically advanced house in 1857, complete with indoor plumbing and a flush toilet. In summer, the rooms are given seasonal 'dress': coverings and netting that protected the inhabitants and furnishings from the elements. There are also intact slave quarters out back – once you see these, you'll recognize them throughout the Quarter.

☎ 525-5661 ✉ 1118-1132 Royal St $ $6/5 ☾ 10am-3:30pm

Labranche Building (6, D4)

Like a veiled maiden, the 1840s Labranche Building is draped with ornate cast-iron work bearing a pattern of leafy tree branches pregnant with acorns. It is said that the tree motif corresponds to the first owner's last name, Labranche. This

An Amazing Resource

The **Preservation Resource Center** (5, E5; ☎ 581-7032; www.prcno.org; 923 Tchoupitoulas St; free; ☾ 9am-4:30pm Mon-Fri, noon-4:30pm Sat; 10 Tchoupitoulas at Andrew Higgins Dr) is a nonprofit organization dedicated to celebrating, restoring and revitalizing the neighborhoods and historic buildings of New Orleans. The vast public area at its offices has displays including detailed ones on the city's neighborhoods. Free guides and walking tour maps are available. The engaging staff will advise you on everything from cycling routes to how to secure low-interest loans to buy and restore your dream shacker.

is a gallicized version of the family's paternal name, Zweig, which in German means 'twig.'

✉ **700 Royal St**

Louisiana State Bank
(6, C5) This imposing structure was designed in 1820 by Benjamin Henry Latrobe, the architect of the south wing of the US Capitol. Notice the bank's monograms (LSB) in the ironwork balcony.

✉ **403 Royal St**

Madame John's Legacy
(6, D4) The architecture and folk-art exhibit are the most interesting aspects of this historic property of the state museum. Built in West Indies style, the 1st floor is made of brick and was used for storage, much like a basement. The living quarters were on the 2nd floor, which is made of wood. Somehow the house survived the catastrophic fires of 1788 and 1794. George Washington Cable's 1873 short story 'Tite Poulette,' about a quadroon (a person who is one-quarter Black) known as Madame John, was set in this house.

☎ 568-6968 ⌨ lsm .crt.state.la.us ✉ 632

Old Ursuline Convent

Dumaine St ⑤ $5/4 ⏰ 9am-5pm Tue-Sun ♿ good

Maspero's Exchange
(6, C5) A plaque marks the spot of Pierre Maspero's slave auction and coffeehouse – a combination sick with irony today. The Exchange was selected as a headquarters for the local militia hastily assembled to aid Andrew Jackson in the fight against the advancing British army; the forces met at Chalmette (2, F3).

✉ **440 Chartres St**

Peychaud's Pharmacy
(6, C5) Back when apothecaries let blood and sold voodoo potions, AA Peychaud, a French refugee from Haiti, earned a reputation with his distinctive cure-all. He mixed his patented bitters recipe (known today as Peychaud's Bitters) with sweeter liquors in a double-sided egg cup known as a *coquetier,* eventually rendered as 'cocktail.' Think of that the next time you stop by a bar for your 'medicine.'

✉ **437 Royal St**

Pitot House Museum
(4, B4) Designed to encourage air circulation, Creole houses typically have double-pitched roofs with dormer windows, louvered-shuttered doors, and interior rooms that open into each other (without a main corridor). This 1799 French-colonial plantation house is an excellent example of the style and takes its name from James Pitot, the first mayor of the incorporated city of New

Orleans. The deeply shaded grounds are a good place for a break.

☎ 482-0312 ⌨ www .pitothouse.org ✉ 1440 Moss St ⑤ $5/2 ⏰ 10am-3pm Wed-Sat 🚌 48 Esplanade to Moss St 🚋 City Park

Old Ursuline Convent
(6, D4) The French order of Ursuline nuns came to New Orleans in the 1700s to educate the colony's girls and to operate a small hospital. A convent was built for them by the French Colonial Army in 1752, making this the oldest building in the Mississippi Valley. The convent survived the city's fires thanks to the concerted firefighting efforts of the citizenry. If you see any parallels between the barren cells used by the nuns and your New Orleans hotel room, move.

☎ 529-3040 ⌨ www .ursulineneworleans .org ✉ 1100 Chartres St ⑤ $5/2 ⏰ tours on the hr 10am-3pm (except noon) Tue-Fri, 11:15am, 1pm & 2pm Sat & Sun ♿ good

US Customs House (6, C6)
The Egyptian revival US Customs House first housed government offices in 1856. Prior to the Civil War, PGT Beauregard oversaw construction. During the Reconstruction period, the African-American division of the Republican party had its offices here. The marble hall on the 2nd floor is said to be stunning, but only bureaucrats can enjoy it.

✉ **423 Canal St**

PLACES OF WORSHIP

New Orleans's heavily Catholic roots mean that there are scores of churches, many reflecting the city's ethnic origins.

Seek solace from the Big Easy at St Patrick's Church

Christ Church Cathedral (3, G4) Although Protestants have lived in New Orleans since colonial times, there were no official churches until 1805. An ad in the *Louisiana Gazette* invited Protestants to form a congregation, resulting in Christ Church, which by popular vote became Episcopalian. The present church was built in 1886. ☎ 895-6602 ☐ www.cccnola.org ⊠ 2919 St Charles Ave ⑤ by donation ☼ tours after 11am Sun service, 10am-noon, 1pm-3pm Mon & Thu, by appointment Tue, Wed & Fri ⓖ St Charles at Sixth St ⓖ good

Our Lady of Guadeloupe Church (6, B4) During the 1853 yellow fever epidemic, the city struggled to bury the victims within Catholic strictures, and used this chapel as a mortuary. It was rechristened Our Lady of Guadeloupe in 1931. Of the church's patrons saints, there are St Jude (impossible cases), St Michael (police), St Florian (firefighters)

and St Expedite(to hurry things up). ☎ 525-1551 ⊠ 411 N Rampart St ⑤ by donation ☼ 7am-6pm ⓖ good

St Augustine's (6, C3) The second-oldest African-American Catholic Church in the country, St Augustine's opened in 1842. The Sisters of the Holy Family, an order of Black Creole nuns, are depicted in the church's stained-glass windows. Jazz funerals frequently depart from here and pass through the streets of the Tremé en route to the cemetery. ☎ 525-5934 ⊠ 1210 Governor Nicholls St ⑤ by donation ☼ Sun Mass 10am ⓐ cab or drive ⓖ good

St Patrick's Church (5, D4) The Irish immigrants of the 1830s established this church, one of many in the city that ministered to the recently arrived Europeans. ☎ 525-4413 ☐ www.oldstpatricks.org ⊠ 724 Camp St ⑤ by donation ☼ Sun Mass 8am, 9:30am & 11am ⓖ St Charles at Girod St ⓖ good

St Expedite

The popular legend about New Orleans' unofficial patron saint, St Expedite, demonstrates the city's true creativity, unhindered by the rigors of canonization, and its ability to spin a good yarn. In an unnamed year, a crate packed with statues of saints was delivered to an order of New Orleans nuns. They came across a box marked *spedito,* which they took to mean 'rush' in Italian. Inside was a figurine of what looked like a Roman general, but the nuns had never met this saint. In the spirit of charity, they gave the statue a home on the altar and named him St Expedite, assigning him the job of finding prompt solutions. Because New Orleans is an insular island, St Expedite was soon regarded as the nuns' own creation, never mind that he has been the patron saint of Sicily since the 1700s and that Paris nuns tell a similar creation myth.

PARKS & PUBLIC SPACES

Parks in the city are lush nearly year-round thanks to the subtropical weather. Even if you're pressed for time, enjoy the enormous oaks hung with Spanish moss.

Audubon Park (3, B-C)
Incorporate a stroll through this 400-acre park during a visit to the Audubon Zoo (p32). Between the street-car stop on St Charles Ave and the zoo, a mile-long paved path circles a lagoon teeming with birdlife. Egrets perch on gnarled live oaks, whose boughs dip toward the murky water.
✉ bound by St Charles Ave, Magazine St, Exposition Blvd & Walnut St 🚋 St Charles at Audubon Park

Lafayette Square (5, D3-4) Originally named Place Gravier, this leafy public square was renamed after Lafayette's visit to New Orleans in 1825. It was the gathering place for the American sector of town. Today it hosts free music concerts.
✉ bound by St Charles Ave, N & S Maestri & Camp Sts 🚋 St Charles at Lafayette Sq

Lee Circle (5, D5) At the center of this roundabout is a statue of the Confederate general Robert E Lee facing north, arms crossed, waiting for the Union's next move.
🚋 St Charles at Lee Circle

Louis Armstrong Park (6, C3) Named in honor of New Orleans' famous jazz cornetist, Louis Armstrong Park occupies a green stretch between the French Quarter and the Tremé. Inside the festive arched entrance is Congo Sq, a historic gathering place for slaves; a statue of Louis Armstrong; a bust of Sidney Bechet, a New Orleans–born clarinetist; the popular jazz radio station WWOZ (p13); and cultural and performing arts centers.
✉ entrance at cnr N Rampart St & St Ann St 🕐 daytime only ♿ good

Moonwalk Park (6, D5) The high point here literally is the viewing platform, with its picture-postcard view of Jackson Sq and St Louis Cathedral. Fronting the river is a wide prom-enade giving an unhindered view of the gigantic container ships and plucky tugboats forging along the muddy Mississippi.
✉ river side of Jackson Sq

Riverwalk (5, F4)
Behind the huge Riverwalk Mall, facing the river, this pleasant walkway is lined with informative plaques about the advent and death of river trade and steamboat jazz bands. Benches and chairs allow for plenty of Old Man River contemplation.
✉ entrance at Poydras St 🚋 Riverfront line

Woldenberg Riverfront Park (6, D6)
Seamlessly joining to Moonwalk Park, this green space near the aquarium used to be lined with wharves, and followed the rhythm of the loading or unloading of merchan-dise. Now the park hosts concerts, evening strolls and is the departure point for riverboat cruises.
✉ river side of the Audubon Aquarium of the Americas

Spanish Moss
The tangled Medusa-like plants known as Span-ish moss make their homes in the branches of the live oaks in the city's parks. Amazingly, *Tillandsia usneoides* is a member of the pineapple family. The French called it 'Spanish beard,' and the Spanish countered by calling it 'French wig.'

COOKING CLASSES

Learn to cook New Orleans–style while in town and you can avoid withdrawal once you go home.

Cookin' Cajun Cooking School (5, F4) Jambalaya, shrimp Creole and bananas Foster are just some of the dishes that might appear on the menu for this two-hour cooking demonstration. The class exam involves sampling the dishes – so go for an A. Cookin' Cajun is in the Creole delicacies food shop in the Riverwalk Mall. ☎ 586-8832 💻 www .cookincajun.com ✉ 1 Poydras St, Riverwalk Mall 💲 $20/10 🕐 class times vary 🚋 Riverfront at Riverwalk Mall ♿ good

New Orleans School of Cooking (6, C5) A lot of humor and a dash of attitude get stirred into the pot during these cooking demonstrations. Participants get to eat the lesson plan of gumbo, jambalaya, bread pudding and pralines, washed down with an Abita beer. Shorter classes are held in the afternoon. You can also arrange classes where you cook rather than watch. ☎ 525-2665 💻 www .nosoc.com ✉ 524 St Louis St 💲 3hr class $25, 2hr class $20 🕐 10am-1pm & 2-4pm ♿ good

Pinch da Tail, Suck da Head

Louisiana's official state crustacean is the crawfish, which back home you probably know as crayfish. Cajuns call them *écrevisses*, and many rural folks just call them mudbugs.

The key to tasty crawfish is boiling them live and using a good spicy boil made with red pepper and other seasonings. It takes a 7lb platter to yield about a single pound of tail meat. Real dives even provide tables with a disposal hole in the middle for the wasted head and shell.

However first you have to peel the little fella. First, grab and uncurl the crawfish, snapping the head and body from the tail. Hold the tail with both hands, using your thumb and finger to crack the tail open and pinch out the meat. As an option, you can suck the head to taste the flavorful 'fat' from the orange-colored hepatopancreas organ. You don't get your stripes until you've sucked the head.

Cook up a storm and make a mess in someone else's kitchen

QUIRKY NEW ORLEANS

Saying 'quirky New Orleans' is almost an oxymoron.

Canal St Ferry (6, D6)

Aboard this state-run ferry, you can take a free ride from New Orleans across the river to the west-bank suburb of Algiers. If it wasn't for the hum of the ferry's motor, you might swear the river did all the work. You can't beat this ride for feeling the power of the Mississippi. Ride this over to Blaine Kern's Mardi Gras World (p32).

✉ **foot of Canal St at Mississippi River** $ **free** ☽ **5:45am-midnight, every half-hr** ♿ **good**

Harrah's New Orleans (5, E3)

This vast casino anchors the old riverfront area in the CBD. With a faux Mardi Gras theme, Harrah's has the standard array of casino bells and whistles, with

Just another day on the streets of New Orleans

100 tables and 2000 slots, complimentary drinks and bargain buffets.

☎ 533-6000 🖥 www .harrahs.com ✉ cnr Canal & N Peters Sts $ free to watch, otherwise... ☽ 24hr 🚊 Riverfront at Canal St ♿ good

J&M Music Shop (6, C4)

Now Hula Mae's Laundromat, the former J&M Music Shop is where R&B legends such as Fats Domino and Dave Bartholomew recorded in the 1950s. A makeshift exhibit of historic photos can be found inside near the dryers.

☎ 522-1336 ✉ 840 N Rampart St ☽ 10am-9pm $ free

New Orleans Historic Voodoo Museum (6, D4)

This small museum has simple but authentic displays of voodoo historical figures, such as Marie Laveau, voodoo altars dedicated to Papa La Bas and the spirit of

Storyville

Like every rough and tumble port city, New Orleans had (correction, has) prostitution. The brothels were so popular that even the politicians publicly acknowledged their existence. In an attempt to regulate the trade, city official Sidney Story proposed a legalized but contained red-light district in 1897 to occupy the lakeside portion of the French Quarter. A modern-day Gomorrah flourished and adopted the do-gooder's name, Storyville. Pimps, madams, drug pushers and moonlighting musicians caroused in this fabled city. Jazz is said to have sprung from its dens, where the classical pianos and horns were ragged with lusty expression. The district was finally closed down by navy orders in 1917 to protect young recruits. To further erase the legend, the houses were razed in 1940 and a housing project was erected in their place.

the Louisiana swamp. A little educational, a little devotional, this collection was founded by Charles Gandolfo, whose grandfather was cured of lockjaw by a voodoo priestess. The 217 N Peters St location has additional exhibits. A look through the gift shop is an experience in itself.
☎ 523-7685 ✉ 724 Dumaine St $ $7/3.50 ⏰ 10am-8pm ♿ good

New Orleans Pharmacy Museum (6, D5) Leeches swimming in an enclosed jar greet visitors, while instruments of torture sit silently in display cases at this 19th-century relic. Dusty voodoo potions occupy another shelf. Upstairs exhibits explain the scientific aspects of the city's multiple epidemics. Recent revamps have added a lot of signage that puts the leeches in their place – medically that is.
☎ 565-8027 🖥 www .pharmacymuseum .org ✉ 514 Chartres St $ $5/4 ⏰ 10am-5pm Tue-Sun

Royal Pharmacy (6, D4) In a blissfully quiet part of Royal St, this 100-year-old pharmacy is an uncluttered space where prescriptions are filled and packs of gum are sold. Its fame comes from the perfectly preserved 1950s soda fountain that peacefully rests along the back wall, just waiting the call to serve a new generation.
☎ 523-5401 ✉ 1101 Royal St $ free ⏰ 9am-5pm Mon-Sat

Voodoo Spiritual Temple (6, C4) Priestess Miriam does African bone readings and palm readings for open-minded seekers. Just across the street from Congo Sq, where many early voodoo rituals were held, her small shop also sells the requisite voodoo objects and dolls.
☎ 522-9627 🖥 www .voodoospiritualtemple .org ✉ 828 N Rampart St ⏰ 10am-5pm

Voodoo

In New Orleans, voodoo remains a powerful force in the lives of many. Clientele hail from all segments of society searching for love or wealth, or wanting to get rid of noisy neighbors. Voodoo priestesses have been called on to help rid neighborhoods of crime or to reverse the fortune of the cursed football team.

In the African animist tradition, godlike spirits freely interacted with the observable world. As this cosmology traveled from Africa to Haiti and beyond to Louisiana, it merged with other rituals and customs to become what is regarded today as voodoo.

The gods of voodoo are called loa and are arranged in a hierarchy with assigned tasks and bribable tastes. Legba guards the gate between the human and spiritual worlds, and can bestow favors to humans in exchange for meat and rum. As pressure grew for slaves to Christianize, Louisiana voodoo adopted Catholic saints as gods and added their statues to revered altars. Voodoo also encompasses the folk traditions of herbal healing; potions (gris-gris) are concocted to heal bones, improve relationships and exact revenge.

Lotions and potions for health, wealth and love

NEW ORLEANS FOR CHILDREN

Kids can find their own Bourbon Street at several delightful places around the Big Easy.

Audubon Aquarium of the Americas (5, F3)

All sorts of fish make an appearance at this cool aquarium covering aquatic life from North and South America. Menacing sharks, rain-forest fish bigger than New York City apartments, sea dragons resembling weeds – all survey their watery homes. Is a starfish spiny? Visit one of the touch pools to find out. During the school year, the aquarium is quieter in the afternoon; during the summer, the morning is best. Combination tickets for entry to the plethora of Audubon sights are available. See p19 for more on the Audubon empire.
☎ 581-4629 🖳 www.auduboninstitute.org ✉ 1 Canal St 💲 $15/8 ⏱ 9:30am-6pm Sun-Thu, 9:30am-7pm Fri & Sat (closes one hr earlier in summer) 🚃 Riverfront line ♿ good

Monkey Hill

Excluding the Mississippi Levee, New Orleans' highest landmass is Monkey Hill, inside the Audubon Zoo. Monkey Hill was built in 1933 as part of a federal works project to give New Orleans children the experience of 'elevation.' Once you're acclimated to New Orleans' flat geography, the 27½-ft hill seems quite monstrous and its modest view is breathtaking.

Audubon Zoo (3, B5)

The zoo is touted as one of the best in the world. The 350 species are divided into creatively landscaped sections. The Central America section, which houses jaguars, is connected by narrow paths littered with faux Mayan sculptures; elephants inhabit the Asian exhibit with knockoff Khmer ruins. However easily the most entertaining is the Louisiana Swamp exhibit, decorated with rusty cars and spotlight-loving raccoons in a mock 1930s setting.
☎ 861-2537 🖳 www.auduboninstitute.org ✉ 6500 Magazine St 💲 $11/6 ⏱ 9:30am-5pm, to 6pm on weekends in summer ⛴ Zoo cruise from Aquarium of the Americas 🚃 St Charles at Audubon Park to free shuttle bus ♿ good

Blaine Kern's Mardi Gras World

The huge heads leering at you from the street tell you you've entered a different world. Blaine Kern's artists have been making Mardi Gras floats since 1947. Warehouse studio tours visit artists working on next

Experience a natural high at Blaine Kern's Mardi Gras World

year's floats, which are made of Styrofoam and papier mâché, and parade mainstays like the 240-ft-long float with tens of thousands of fiber-optic lights.

☎ 361-7821 ⏹ www .mardigrasworld.com ✉ 233 Newton St, Algiers ⓢ $13.50/6.50 ⏱ 9:30am-4:30pm ⚓ Canal St ferry to free shuttle bus

Carousel Gardens (4, B4)
A renovated 1906 carousel with a working Wurlitzer organ and stained-glass cupola is this garden's centerpiece. There are also amusement rides.

☎ 482-4888 ⏹ www .neworleanscitypark .com ✉ cnr Esplanade Ave & Wisner Blvd ⓒ entry $2, extra for rides ⏱ usually 11am-6pm Sat & Sun, hours vary Dec, Jan & Mar, May-Aug, closed Feb

House of Broel (3, H3)
Drooling over dolls comes naturally at this bridal-shop-cum-fantasyland. A vast dollhouse collection includes 15 large houses – think antebellum mansions – and more than 50 additional vignettes populated by miniature Rhetts and Scarletts. This is not the place to come for Barbies and Kens.

☎ 522-2220 ✉ 2220 St Charles Ave ⓢ $10/5 ⏱ 10am-5pm Mon-Sat ⓑ St Charles at Jackson Ave

Louisiana Children's Museum (5, E4)
Guaranteed to bring out the kid in anyone, this place has a big bubble maker and a grocery store with plastic foodstuffs and play cash registers. There's a café with a toy kitchen, where kids cook up plastic dishes. Kids can pretend to be news anchors or the pilot of a tugboat. Are you beat? Your kids aren't.

☎ 523-1357 ⏹ www .lcm.org ✉ 420 Julia St ⓢ $7 ⏱ 9:30am-4:30pm Tue-Sat, noon-4:30pm Sun ⏹ 10 Tchoupitoulas at Julia St ⓖ good

Musée Conti Wax Museum (6, C5)
What's better than reading about history? Seeing the players rendered in wax. Heroes, emperors and even monsters are always watching you out of the corners of their eyes. And who knew that Napoleon liked to sign away large tracts of land from the comfort of his bathtub?

☎ 525-2605 ⏹ www .get-waxed.com ✉ 917 Conti St ⓢ $6.75/5.75 ⏱ 10am-5pm Mon-Sat, noon-5pm Sun ⓖ good

Southern Fossil & Mineral Exchange (3, J4)
Part museum, part nightmare and part store, the Exchange is chock full of taxidermy, including

Children's Museum flag

a gaping stuffed alligator, and display cases of skulls from critters large and small. If you've failed with the rabbit's foot, an alligator key chain might bring some bayou luck. And for those looking for something a little more mundane, there are cases of colorful rocks.

☎ 523-5525 ✉ 2049 Magazine St ⓢ free ⏱ noon-5pm Sat ⏹ 11 Magazine at Sophie Wright Pl

Storyland (4, B4)
Popular children's fairytales have been translated into a playground at this delightful place, set in City Park, that also holds puppet shows.

☎ 482-4888 ⏹ www .neworleanscitypark.com ✉ cnr Esplanade Ave & Wisner Blvd ⓢ $3/free ⏱ usually 10am-5pm Sat & Sun, hours vary Oct-Dec & Mar-Sep

Babysitting Services
Most major hotels offer on-site babysitting services and extra bedding for children. Smaller and more modest lodgings are also familiar with parents' needs and can usually provide the name of recommended child-minding services. If you need to stow the youngsters for a few hours, consider inquiring about these services when making hotel reservations.

Out & About

WALKING TOURS
French Quarter

This tour is a sampler of Spanish, French and American architecture. Start at Jackson Sq. Go downriver along Chartres St to Dumaine St, and turn left to **Madame John's Legacy** (**1**; p26), an example of West Indies–style architecture. Backtrack to Chartres and head toward Ursulines Ave. **Old Ursuline Convent** (**2**; p26), is the Quarter's oldest structure, dating to 1752. Take Ursulines Ave to Royal St and turn left; the **Cornstalk Hotel** (**3**; ☎ 523-1515; 915 Royal St) is named for its 1859 cornstalk-motif fence. In the 800 block of Royal St, notice the oval

distance 1 mile **duration** 1hr
▶ **start** cnr St Ann & Chartres Sts
● **end** cnr St Peter & Chartres Sts

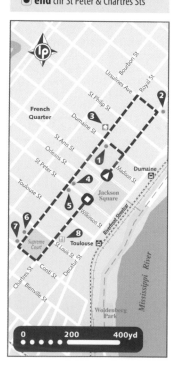

Glass door detail at the Cornstalk Hotel

coverings along the building foundations: these are 'weep' holes for air circulation. Continue to the **Labranche Building** (**4**; p25) and its photogenic balconies. Stop at the **LeMonnier Mansion** (**5**; No 640) to pick out the initials in the cast-iron work. The cocktail was invented at **Peychaud's Pharmacy** (**6**; p26). **Louisiana State Bank** (**7**; p26) is an American adaptation of original Spanish styles. Turn left at Conti St and go past Exchange Alley, once home to famous fencing masters. Turn left at Chartres St and walk to **Napoleon House** (**8**; p51), named in honor of the French emperor. From here Jackson Sq is two blocks downriver.

Garden District

During New Orleans' golden age, wealthy Americans built Greek Revival miniplantations upriver from the old French Quarter. Take the streetcar from Canal St to Jackson Ave and head toward the river. At 1410 Jackson Ave, the Greek-columned **Buckner House** (**1**) was built for a cotton merchant in 1856. Turn right on to Chestnut for two blocks, then left onto First St. At 1239 First St, novelist Anne Rice once lived in **Rosegate** (**2**), named for its rose-motif cast-iron fence. Continue left for one block to the corner of Camp St. In 1889, Confederate President Jefferson Davis died at **Payne-Strachan House** (**3**; 1134 First St).

Wet your whistle at Commander's Palace

Backtrack on First St to 2343 Prytania St, where **Louise S McGehee School** (**4**) occupies an 1872 renaissance mansion designed by James Freret. Turn left to get to the outdoor **chapel** (**5**; 2521 Prytania St) of Our Lady of Perpetual Help. At No 2605, James Gallier designed the 1849 **Charles Briggs House** (**6**), unique for its Gothic windows and Elizabethan chimneys. At the corner of Prytania and Fourth Sts, **Colonel Short's Villa** (**7**; 1448 Fourth St) is guarded by a cornstalk fence – look closer for morning glories, pumpkins and wheat. Continue to Washington Ave; turn left to explore **Lafayette Cemetery No 1** (**8**; p20) and have a meal at **Commander's Palace** (**9**; p56) or turn right to catch the streetcar downtown.

distance 1 mile **duration** 1½hr
▶ **start** 🚋 St Charles Ave at Jackson Ave
◉ **end** 🚋 St Charles Ave at Washington Ave

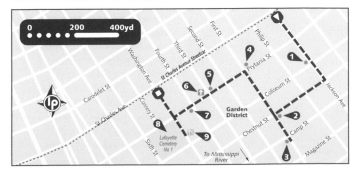

St Charles Streetcar

From the comfort of a window seat on the St Charles streetcar, you can tour New Orleans' uptown neighborhoods. The only walking you'll do here is from the firebox to your seat. At Canal and Carondelet Sts, catch the streetcar heading uptown. At Lafayette Sq, the Greek Revival building on the left is **Gallier Hall** (**1**; 545 St Charles Ave), the former city hall. Just past the roundabout, named **Lee Circle** (**2**; p28) in honor of the Confederate general, begins the Garden District. On the right, at the corner of Sixth St, **Christ Church Cathedral** (**3**, p27) was built in 1886 to serve the city's Protestant inhabitants. At Louisiana Ave, you cross into Uptown District, where the mansions get

Grecian greatness at Gallier Hall

grander. For a quick drink, hop off at the **Columns Hotel** (**4**; p62). Nearby streets (Austerlitz, Constantinople, Marengo, Milan and Jena) celebrate Napoleonic victories. **Sacred Heart Academy** (**5**), a girls' school, is on the right at Jena St. On the left, at Soniat St, the neo-Italianate **mansion** (**6**) now houses a branch of the public library. On the right at No 5809 is a gorgeous mansion known as the **Wedding Cake House** (**7**). **Loyola** (**8**) and **Tulane Universities** (**9**) approach on the right after Calhoun St. Across the street

distance 12 miles round trip
duration 3hr
▶ **start** 🚋 Carondelet & Canal Sts
● **end** 🚋 Carondelet & Canal Sts

is **Audubon Park** (**10**; p28). Hop off the streetcar at S Carrollton Ave for a bite at **Camellia Grill** (**11**; p56); catch the streetcar going in the opposite direction to return.

DAY TRIPS
River Road Plantations &
Barataria Preserve
(1, D1, E2, F2)

Preserved antebellum sugar plantations set along the curving course of the Mississippi River: doesn't it sound tranquil and romantic? Well if you look past some rather large chemical plants, and ignore the fact that the series of highways collectively referred to as the 'River Road' are shielded from views of the Mississippi by 15ft- to 24ft-tall grassy embankments, then you might just find this day to be a real joy.

Don't miss the 1805 **Laura Plantation**, a well-preserved West Indies–style building with an impeccable family history and interesting descriptions of Creole customs. A fire in 2004 caused heavy damage but it is still the pick of the plantation crop. As a counterpoint, visit one (or two) of the American plantations. **Nottoway** (1849–59) is probably the best mix of history and architectural detail, but it is also the farthest from New Orleans. **Oak Alley** has its irresistible avenue of live oaks, but the tour is like a *Gone with the Wind* nightmare, and you may not give a damn. The Gothic steamboat-era **San Francisco Plantation** is as outrageous as the city with which it shares a name.

Escape the clash of yesterday and today at **Barataria Preserve**, a national park where you can plunge headlong into the prehistoric beauty of Louisiana's swamps. During the 8 miles (13km) of hiking trails, you will pass intimately close to sleeping alligators masquerading as gnarled logs, stoic fishing egrets and sunbathing turtles – the bigger the splash, the bigger the 'gator.

Travel to and from each of these day trips is best done by car.

INFORMATION

Plantations
12-60 miles (19-97km) northwest of New Orleans
- 🚗 car
- ✉ Laura Plantation (☎ 225-265-7690; www.lauraplantation.com; 2247 Hwy 18); Nottoway Plantation (☎ 225-545-2730; www.nottoway.com; 30970 Hwy 1); Oak Alley (☎ 225-265-2151; www.oakalleyplantation.com; 3645 Hwy 18); San Francisco Plantation (☎ 985-535-2341; www.sanfranciscoplantation.org; 2646 Hwy 44)
- 💲 $10/5
- 🕙 9am-5pm
- ℹ tickets purchased on-site

Barataria Preserve
20 miles (32km) south of New Orleans
- 🚗 car
- 🖥 www.nps.gov
- 💲 free
- ℹ National Park Service Visitors Center (☎ 504-589-2330; Hwy 3134)
- 🕙 9am-5pm

Enter if you dare: Oak Alley Plantation

Cajun Country: St Martinville, Breaux Bridge & Lafayette (1, C1)

In 1755 French settlers living in Acadia, present-day Nova Scotia, were expelled by the new British overseers. What ensued is memorialized in the people's history as Le Grande Dérangement, when Acadian families were uprooted and wandered the US and Europe in exile. In 1785, seven boatloads of refugees arrived in Louisiana and made their way to the uninhabited swamps and prairies. More Acadians followed, eventually establishing a new homeland and a modified identity: Cajun.

On the banks of the Bayou Teche, two legendary Acadian lovers were said to have been briefly reunited under the boughs of the majestic **Evangeline Oak** in St Martinville; Longfellow's 1847 epic poem 'Evangeline' was inspired by the bittersweet tale, and French is still spoken in this charming town. **St Martinville Cultural Heritage Center** recounts the histories of brothers in exile: the Acadians and Africans of southern Louisiana.

Lafayette, the self-crowned capital of Cajun Country, offers visitors more cultural attractions. A healthy education on Acadiana can be found at the folklife museum of **Vermilionville** and the National Parks Service's **Acadian Cultural Center**. A survey of the nightlife can be found in the city's many zydeco clubs.

If you're too beat to make it back to New Orleans, lay down beside the mythic waters of Bayou Teche in nearby Breaux Bridge. Overlooking the swift current, **Bayou Cabins**, which started out as a modest boudin and cracklin' shop, has nine rustic cabins salvaged from Cajun homesteads.

INFORMATION

120 miles (193km) west of New Orleans

🚗 car

✉ St Martinville Cultural Heritage Center (☎ 337-394-2273; 121 New Market St); Vermilionville (☎ 337-233-4077; 1600 Surrey St); Acadian Cultural Center (☎ 337-232-0789; www.nps.gov; 501 Fisher Rd at Surrey St; ⌚ 8am-5pm); Bayou Cabins (☎ 337-332-6158; www.bayoucabins.com; 100 Mills Ave/Hwy 94)

⌚ most sites 10am-4pm; Vermilionville closed Mon

ℹ St Martinville Tourist Information Center (☎ 337-394-2233; 215 Evangeline Blvd); Lafayette Convention & Visitors Bureau (☎ 337-232-3737; www.lafayettetravel.com); Bayou Teche Visitors Center (☎ 337-332-8500; 314 E. Bridge St)

✖ Mulate's (☎ 337-332-4648; 325 Mills Ave/Hwy 94, Breaux Bridge)

The famed Evangeline Oak

ORGANIZED TOURS

French Quarter Walking Tours Friends of the Cabildo give two-hour tours of French Quarter architecture and history – with a dose of hard fiction – including free admission to two historic museums. Although no reservations are needed, arrive 10 minutes before departure.
☎ 523-3939 ⬛ www.frenchquartertour.com ✉ 523 St Ann St $ $12 ☽ 1:30pm Mon, 10am & 1:30pm Tue-Sun

Gay Heritage Tour Robert Batson leads groups through the French Quarter, dispensing historical and humorous stories of local characters, including Tennessee Williams. Tours depart from the Alternatives Shop.
☎ 945-6789 ✉ 909 Bourbon St $ $20 for 4 people or more ☽ 1pm Wed & Sat

Heritage Literary Tour More than 65 noted authors have lived and written in New Orleans, leaving behind oral histories conveyed to you on this tour by Dr Kenneth Holditch, professor of literature at the University of New Orleans. Tours can be tailored to specific interests or authors.
☎ 949-9805 ✉ 732 Frenchmen St $ $20 ☽ by appointment

Honey Island Swamp Tours Led by ecologist Dr Paul Wagner, these nature tours put visitors in small boats to get back into the deep recesses of this primeval swamp, which lies across the seemingly endless length of the I-10 Lake Pontchartrain bridge. The tours explore various parts of the 250-square-mile swamp.
☎ 985-641-1769 ⬛ www.honeyisland swamp.com ✉ Crawford Landing, 106 Holly Ridge Dr, Slidell $ $20/12, $25 hotel pick-up ☽ call to check tour times

Le Monde Créole Laura Locoul grew up on a Mississippi River sugar plantation. Thanks to her detailed diary, much is known about her life and the times. This 2½-hour tour explores the French Quarter sites of her diary. Among the fascinating aspects explored is the fact that Creole culture – unlike the rest of the South – was class- rather than color-based.
☎ 568-1801 ⬛ www.lemondecreole.com ✉ 624 Royal St $ $20/15 ☽ 10:30am & 1:30pm Mon-Sat, 10am & 1:30pm Sun, reservations required

Mr Denny's Voyageur Swamp Tour With an uncanny resemblance to Dennis Hopper, Mr Denny leads two-hour, 8-mile (13km) canoe trips through Honey Island Swamp, gliding right up to sunbathing alligators and shimmying into moss-canopied slews. Expect a fair bit of cultural and ecological info to go with your paddling.
☎ 985-643-4839 ⬛ www.gator-den.com ✉ 55344 Hwy 90 E, Slidell $ $20/12, $25 hotel pick-up ☽ call to check tour times

Save Our Cemeteries, Inc The purpose of these tours shouldn't be any surprise. They are easily the best way to get into the city's weird, wild and just plain spooky cemeteries. The nonprofit group works to preserve and protect these surprisingly fragile sites. Make your choice between tours of St Louis Cemetery No 1 and Lafayette Cemetery No 1.
☎ 525-3377 ⬛ www.saveourcemeteries.org $ $6-12 ☽ call for details on tour starting points & times

Steamboat Natchez Cruise The *Natchez* plies the Mississippi River – two-hour daytime cruises enjoy an onboard calliope organist, while two-hour evening cruises are serenaded by a Dixieland jazz band. It's the one real steamboat operating out of New Orleans, and a tour of the hissing and aromatic engine room is worth the price alone.
☎ 586-8777 ⬛ www.neworleanssteamboat.com ✉ Toulouse St wharf, across from Jackson Sq $ $18.50/9.25 daytime cruise, $30/15 evening jazz cruise, meals extra ☽ 11:30am, 2:30pm & 6pm

Shopping

Shopping in New Orleans is hell for franchisers and heaven for those looking for reasons to buy an extra bag for the trip home. The mad profusion of shops is only matched by the mad profusion of goods inside. Designers, collectors, importers and artists all have their places.

You can buy works of art – good and bad, genuine and fake; frocks new and frocks old; treasures from attics and trash from the basement. Some shops simply defy description and are a riot of stuff you just won't find anywhere else. For the jazz collector, a music shop may be a pilgrimage, while a hot sauce hound may find nirvana in a market.

Expect to find anything and everything for sale in New Orleans. Finding it all is half the fun.

SHOPPING AREAS

Refined **Royal St** has been a shopping venue since the mid-19th century. Creole families maintained their Frenchness through acquisitions of the latest rococo or Louis XV revival styles. The air of sophistication is still present today thanks to the street's architectural beauty and the numerous galleries and antique dealers centered on the blocks between Iberville and St Ann Sts. During business hours, portions of Royal St are closed to automobile traffic, further heightening the European feel.

The **French Market** (6, E4; p11) and almost the entire length of Decatur St deal, primarily to the tourist crowd, in classic and tawdry New Orleans souvenirs.

Magazine St runs roughly parallel to the river, from Canal St to Audubon Park, passing through the Garden Districts and Uptown. At major avenues separating the different neighborhoods, clusters of eclectic shops reflect the tastes and attitudes of the nearby residents. Start at one end in the morning and finish at the other and you'll wonder where all your time and money went.

Julia St anchors the mainstream galleries of the Warehouse district, but you can find artistic treasures from makeshift stands on Jackson Sq to vacant lots in Bywater.

If you want good views of the action on the river – or just some air-conditioning – the **Riverwalk Mall** (5, F4) is well stocked with national chains and souvenir stores.

Shop 'til you drop on Magazine St

FASHION & JEWELRY

House of Lounge (3, J4)
A homegrown version of Victoria's Secret, House of Lounge gives boudoir fashion an injection of glamour. Ladies' dainties, men's smoking jackets and feathered slippers would be perfect for lounging around the house or sipping martinis. Go on, buy the feather boa.
☎ 671-8300 ✉ 2044 Magazine St ☼ 10am-6pm Mon-Sat, noon-5pm Sun ☒ 11 Magazine at Sophie Wright Pl

Il Negozio (3, F5)
Annoyed by closet-sized boutiques with a selection of three dresses all in size zero? This stylish store actually has a good assortment of dresses, skirts, pants and blouses. What's more, it's in a charming old house with a real fitting room and a lush garden out front to cool your heels – and wallet.
☎ 269-0130 ✉ 3607 Magazine St ☼ 10am-

5pm Tue-Sat ☒ 11 Magazine at Foucher St

Meyer the Hatter (5, E2)
Since 1894, Meyer the Hatter has been selling fashions for the head. First, Stetson was all the rage, followed by Borsalino and now Dobbs and Kangol. This will be one of the best hat stores you're likely to find anywhere.
☎ 525-1048 ✉ 120 St Charles Ave ☼ 10am-5:45pm Mon-Sat

Mignon Faget (3, F5)
Local artist Mignon Faget creates contemporary jewelry influenced by Louisiana flora and architecture. Medallion earrings, twig bracelets, tulip pendants and fleur-de-lis rings featuring semiprecious stones have won her international attention.
☎ 891-2005 ✉ 3801 Magazine St ☼ 10am-6pm Mon-Sat ☒ 11 Magazine at General Taylor St

Molly McNamara Designs

Molly McNamara Designs (3, J4) Pendants mimicking aboveground tombs or earrings evoking the curve of an oyster shell. Molly McNamara crafts New Orleans–inspired jewelry in this fun Lower Garden District shop.
☎ 566-1100 ✉ 2128 Magazine St ☼ 10am-5pm Tue-Sat ☒ 11 Magazine at Sophie Wright Pl

Thomas Mann Gallery (3, J4) Look here for amazing metalwork, whether it's jewelry or designer items. Mann's styles are

CLOTHING & SHOE SIZES

Women's Clothing

Aust/UK	8	10	12	14	16	18
Europe	36	38	40	42	44	46
Japan	5	7	9	11	13	15
USA	6	8	10	12	14	16

Women's Shoes

Aust/USA	5	6	7	8	9	10
Europe	35	36	37	38	39	40
France only	35	36	38	39	40	42
Japan	22	23	24	25	26	27
UK	3½	4½	5½	6½	7½	8½

Men's Clothing

Aust	92	96	100	104	108	112
Europe	46	48	50	52	54	56

	S	M	M		L	
Japan						
UK/USA	35	36	37	38	39	40

Men's Shirts (Collar Sizes)

Aust/Japan	38	39	40	41	42	43
Europe	38	39	40	41	42	43
UK/USA	15	15½	16	16½	17	17½

Men's Shoes

Aust/UK	7	8	9	10	11	12
Europe	41	42	43	44½	46	47
Japan	26	27	27.5	28	29	30
USA	7½	8½	9½	10½	11½	12½

Measurements approximate only; try before you buy.

a blend of techno and romance, and the workmanship is exquisite.
☎ 581-2113 ✉ 1804 Magazine St ⏰ 10am-6pm Mon-Sat 🚌 11 Magazine at Felicity St

Town & Country (3, J3)
Society maids and maidens come here for classic-style wedding dresses, ball gowns and other high-end frocks.
☎ 523-7027 ✉ 1514 St Charles Ave ⏰ 10am-6pm Mon-Sat 🚋 St Charles at MLK Blvd

Trashy Diva (3, J4) More diva than trashy, this Magazine St boutique specializes in 1920s nightclub wear. Steel-boned corsets, classic-style chokers and feather boas are fun to play dress-up with. You'll find a second outlet at 829 Chartres St.
☎ 581-4555 🖥 www .trashydiva.com ✉ 2048 Magazine St ⏰ noon-6pm 🚌 11 Magazine at Sophie Wright Pl

Victoria's Designer Shoes (6, D5) Mundane shoe mavens look elsewhere. It's

straps and heels, sequins and stilettos that grace feet with sex appeal at Victoria's.
☎ 568-9990 ✉ 532 Chartres St ⏰ 10am-6pm

Violet's (6, D4)
Everything from jewelry and shawls to gowns can be found here, all designed by locals on the move. Check out the casual stuff with more flair than just about anywhere.
☎ 569-0088 ✉ 808 Chartres St ⏰ 10am-6pm, much later Feb-May

ANTIQUES & INTERESTING JUNK

Antiques & Things (3, H4)
Vintage lamps, tables, dishes and rugs simulate the early 1960s in all their thin-tie, organ-jazz glory. This antique mall gives you a foray into make-believe.
☎ 897-9466 ✉ 2855 Magazine St ⏰ 10am-5pm Mon-Sat, noon-5pm Sun 🚌 11 Magazine at Washington Ave

Christopher's Discoveries (3, H4) This is the kind of shop that makes Magazine St such fun. There's a mix of old and new jewelry, decorator items and local artworks.
☎ 899-6226 ✉ 2842 Magazine St ⏰ 10am-6pm Mon-Sat 🚌 11 Magazine at Washington Ave

Jean Bragg Antiques (3, F5) Even those with only a vague interest in Southern art will enjoy a visit to the city's premier collection of

regional works. Look for the landscapes by painter Knute Heldner, the bulbous pots of George Ohr, and Arts-and-Crafts pottery from New Orleans' Newcomb College. Even the air here is refined.
☎ 895-7375 ✉ 3901 Magazine St ⏰ 10am-5pm Mon-Sat 🚌 11 Magazine at General Taylor

Keil's Antiques (6, C5)
Search three floors of French and English antiques for a treasure, maybe a dining-room or bedroom suite, a mirror or a chandelier?
☎ 522-4552 ✉ 325 Royal St ⏰ 9am-5pm Mon-Sat

Lucullus Culinary Antiques, Art & Objects (6, D5) Owner Patrick Dunne is an advocate of using, not collecting, culinary antiques. Follow his advice and add more ritual and elegance to your life with an antique café au lait bowl, or an

absinthe spoon for creating the evening's cocktail.
☎ 528-9620 ✉ 610 Chartres St ⏰ 9:30am-5pm Mon-Sat

Moss Antiques (6, C5) This fourth-generation dealer specializes in 19th-century chandeliers and antique jewelry, inkwells and cigar humidors. Perfect items if you want your New Orleans memento to be more lasting than a strand of beads.
☎ 522-3981 ✉ 411 Royal St ⏰ 9am-5pm Mon-Sat

MS Rau Antiques (6, D5)
The oldest of the Royal St antique stores, MS Rau has a large collection of European and American antiques. The store's rare furniture, porcelain objets d'art and Louisiana jewelry outpaces many museum collections.
☎ 523-5660 ✉ 630 Royal St ⏰ 9am-5:15pm Mon-Sat

ARTS & CRAFTS

**Anton Haardt Gallery
(3, H4)** Artists here include the self-taught Mose Tolliver, who used to hang his paintings on trees in his front yard. Future gallery owner Anton Haardt took an interest, and bought one, then another, until he had a small collection and later this small business. Also look for Sybil Gibson's paintings on grocery bags.
☎ 891-9080 ✉ 2858 Magazine St ⏰ 11am-5pm Tue-Sat 🚌 11 Magazine at Washington Ave

Ariodante (5, D4) The traditional crafts of mask making, glassblowing and ceramics get modern interpretations at this gallery.
☎ 524-3233 ✉ 535 Julia St ⏰ 11am-5pm Mon-Sat 🚋 St Charles at Julia St

**Arthur Roger Gallery
(5, E4)** This gallery features rotating exhibits of local and regional artists. Highlights have included Michael Willmon's surrealistic oil paintings of New Orleans' ghost-riddled cemeteries and Ted Kincaid's thunderheads and other paintings of Southern weather.
☎ 522-1999 ✉ 432 Julia St ⏰ 10am-5pm Tue-Sat 🚌 11 Magazine at Julia St

Bergeron Studio & Gallery (5, E3) Vintage photos of New Orleans and its surrounds are the stars at this fascinating gallery.
☎ 522-7503 ✉ 516 Natchez St ⏰ 10am-5pm Mon-Fri, 10am-4pm Sat

Berta's & Mina's Antiquities (3, F5) Littered with canvases and reeking of paint, this studio displays the playful folk art of Nilo Lanzas, who took up a paint brush at age 63. Custom-painted duck decoys add to the eclectic charm.
☎ 895-6201 ✉ 4138 Magazine St ⏰ 10am-6pm Mon-Sat, 11am-6pm Sun 🚌 11 Magazine at Marengo St

**Bywater Art Market
(2, E2)** In the 1920s the French Quarter was filled with artists living cheaply. It attracted such greats as William Faulkner and Tennessee Williams. Now the Bywater modestly wears this distinction. Among the many notable works are poignant photographs by Christopher Porché West.
☎ 944-7900 ✉ 3301 Chartres St at Piety St ⏰ 9am-4pm 3rd Sat of every month 🚗 cab or drive

A Gallery for Fine Photography (6, C5) The history of photography is cataloged at this gallery of original prints. Rare Storyville scenes by EJ Bellocq and early shots of New Orleans from William Henry Jackson are worth a look.
☎ 568-1313 ✉ 241 Chartres St ⏰ 10am-5pm Tue-Sat

**George Schmidt Gallery
(5, D4)** The city's past unfolds on canvas here with lifelike characters and intriguing subplots. Mardi Gras, jazz musicians and famous parties, all dating from before 1950, have posed as Schmidt's imagined subjects.
☎ 592-0206 ✉ 626 Julia St ⏰ 12:30-4:30pm Tue-Sat 🚋 St Charles at Julia St

**Jonathan Ferrara Gallery
(5, D4)** The fun-loving Ferrara displays his own works and those of his friends in this bright gallery. Works span the gamut of medias.
☎ 522-5471 🖥 www .jonathanferraragallery. com ✉ 841 Carondelet St ⏰ noon-6pm Tue-Sat 🚋 St Charles at Julia St

Scream your head off at George Schmidt Gallery

Skullduggery at Simon's

La Belle Galerie (6, C5)
Photographs of New Orleans' brass bands and acrylics of musicians form a small portion of this polychromatic gallery's big selection of African-American art. Limited edition prints by national artists and Jazz Fest posters are also available.
☎ 529-3080 ⊠ 309 Chartres St ⏲ 10am-7pm

LeMieux Galleries (5, E4)
This large and open space is a fine venue for displaying the works of some of the better known Gulf-coast artists and sculptors. Examples include Deedra D Ludwig's luminous studies of nature's forms and light.
☎ 522-5988 ⊠ 332 Julia St ⏲ 10am-5:30pm Mon-Sat 🚋 St Charles at Julia St

New Orleans School of Glass Works & Printmaking Studio (5, E4) View artists at work in their printmaking, bookbinding and hot glass studios. A range of classes allows you to join in. Learn glassblowing in a day ($210). Pieces made by the artists are sold.
☎ 529-7277 ⊠ 727 Magazine St ⏲ 11am-5pm Mon-Sat 🚌 11 Magazine at Julia St

Photo Works (6, D4) The intricate shadow of a cast-iron balcony, the acrobatic bend in the Mississippi River and the mad throng of people on Bourbon St are preserved in color and in black and white by veteran photographer Louis Sahuc.
☎ 593-9090 ⊠ 839 Chartres St ⏲ 10am-5:30pm Thu-Mon

Rhino Gallery (6, D4) This nonprofit co-op features the work of Louisiana artists in a variety of media. With works like the 'Dirty Girls' (clay pots) you can't go wrong.
☎ 569-8191 ⊠ 927 Royal St ⏲ 10am-6pm Mon-Sat, 11am-6pm Sun

Simon of New Orleans Gallery (3, H4) Affable Simon Hardeveld paints colorful signs with common expressions. The popular New Orleans slogan 'Be Nice or Leave' appears on scrap plywood. His personal favorite is 'Shalom Y'all.' Got a slogan you like? He'll paint it.
☎ 561-0088 ⊠ 2126 Magazine St ⏲ 10am-5pm Thu-Sat 🚌 11 Magazine at Sophie Wright Pl

Stella Jones Gallery (5, D3) African-American, Caribbean and African artworks document the experience of the diaspora through paintings, sculptures and photography. Jones is a dealer in prints from the *Life* magazine collection of African-American images.
☎ 568-9050 ⊠ 201 St Charles Ave, enter on Common St ⏲ 10am-7pm Mon-Fri, noon-7pm Sat

Sylvia Schmidt Gallery (5, E4)
This beautiful gallery specializes in contemporary forms, many entertainingly unconventional. It's a hotspot for recognized local talent.
☎ 522-2000 ⊠ 400a Julia St ⏲ 11am-5pm Tue-Sat 🚋 St Charles at Julia St

---

Cover Art
Next time you beat a path to Bourbon St, take a good look at the sidewalk (or 'banquette' in local parlance) for a water meter cover. Notice the covers decorated with an art deco–style crescent moon and stars? This design was so popular that people would steal the covers, leaving behind gaping holes and a serious public-safety problem. Quick to spot a market, local artists have gotten busy producing copies. Don Wurst at **Old World Casting Co** (3, H4; ☎ 450-1843; 2842 Magazine St; ⏲ 10am-6pm Mon-Sat; 11 Magazine St at Washington Ave) sells copies for $30.

FOOD & DRINK

A&P Grocery (6, D4) This branch of the national chain is the place to go for a huge range of local spices and hot sauces at everyday prices. Want to see what Quarter cooks cook with? Come here.
☎ 523-1353 ✉ 701 Royal St ⏱ 9am-9pm

Bayou Country (6, D5) Hot sauces, Cajun spices, drink mixes, gift baskets and goofy souvenirs are ready to stick with you here like a Hurricane stain on a T-shirt.
☎ 523-3113 ✉ 3rd fl, Jackson Brewery Mall, 600 Decatur St ⏱ 10am-5pm

Central Grocery (6, D4) The muffuletta's birthplace also sells imported goods from Italy, Creole filé powder for sprinkling on gumbo, and seasonings used by all the Louisiana cooks.
☎ 523-1620 ✉ 923 Decatur St ⏱ 8am-5:30pm Mon-Sat, 9am-5:30pm Sun

Laura's Candies (6, D4) Truffles, specialty chocolates and handmade candies are just the gift for a sweet-toothed someone. Laura's Mississippi mud pralines are made with caramel, pecans, and milk or dark chocolate. Dive into the samples.
☎ 525-3880 ✉ 938 Royal St ⏱ 10am-6pm

New Orleans School of Cooking (6, C5) After the show is over, the general store here has a good

selection of Cajun kitchen essentials. Ellis Stansel's gourmet rice, Kevin's seasoning blend and Cajun Power sauce will have you flying back for more.
☎ 525-2665 ✉ 524 St Louis St ⏱ 9:15am-5pm

Southern Candymakers (6, C5) Generous samples allow you to choose just the right kind of praline for the folks back home. Southern's award-winning pralines feature chunky pecans, not the crumbs used by lesser stores. The store also sells

taffy and other candies.
☎ 523-5544 ✉ 334 Decatur St ⏱ 10am-5pm

Vieux Carré Wine & Spirits (6, C5) Top-shelf whiskies, scotches and champagnes will cure whatever ails you. An extensive selection of wines covers the globe, while the best tequilas from across the Gulf of Mexico find a ready, if temporary, home here.
☎ 568-9463 ✉ 422 Chartres St ⏱ 10am-10pm Mon-Sat, 10am-7pm Sun

---

Crescent City Farmer's Market

Every Saturday rain or shine several dozen local farmers, bakers and other artisan cooks sell their goods at this long-running **farmer's market** (5, E4; ☎ 529-7277; www.crescentcityfarmersmarket .org; 700 Magazine St; ⏱ 8am-noon Sat). The event is as much a community gathering as a chance to stock the larder with old friends, sharing news over a cup of chicory (a blend of roasted coffee beans and chicory root, a plant related to endive) coffee. This is a fine spot to sample and buy some of the best local foodstuffs. Expect to rub elbows with some top local chefs while you're at it. A smaller version is held Wednesday lunch at the French Market (6, E4).

Indulge in some mud therapy at Laura's Candies

BOOKS & MUSIC

Beaucoup Books (3, C5)
This Magazine St bookstore draws many contemporary authors for readings, and offers a wide selection of general-interest and regional titles, with excellent recommendations of the latter. ☎ 895-2663 ✉ 5414 Magazine St ⊙ 10am-6pm Mon-Sat, noon-5pm Sun 🚌 11 Magazine at Jefferson Ave

Beckham's Book Store (6, C5) Rare and second-hand books line the walls of this bibliophile's haunt. Classical records, piano rolls and old prints complete the collection. ☎ 522-9875 ✉ 228 Decatur St ⊙ 10am-6pm

Faulkner House (6, D4)
This bookstore (and former residence of William Faulkner) sells rare first editions of Southern writers. Less precious editions of past and present forces in Southern literature are carried as well. Ask who's hot now. ☎ 524-2940 ✉ 624 Pirate's Alley ⊙ 10am-6pm

Jim Russell Records (3, J4) This dusty Lower Garden District shop boasts over a million new and used LPs from Louisiana music to rare rock and obscure blues. The store's strength is its 45s collection. Sample your disk on

the customer turntables before you buy. ☎ 522-2602 ✉ 1837 Magazine St ⊙ 10am-7pm Mon-Sat, 1-6pm Sun 🚌 11 Magazine at Sophie Wright Pl

Louisiana Music Factory (6, C6) From R&B to Dixieland, Louisiana Music Factory has one of the widest selections of regional music in the city. Listening stations for both CDs and vinyl allow you to test drive new and used products before you buy. This is *the* reason to come to New Orleans for many a collector and fan. ☎ 586-1094 ✉ 210 Decatur St ⊙ 10am-7pm Mon-Sat, 11am-7pm Sun

Octavia Books (3, C5) In a stunningly bright and airy space, Octavia Books is one of the city's best general-interest bookstores. Local selections are many and the travel section is good. ☎ 899-7323 ✉ 513 Octavia St ⊙ 10am-6pm Mon-Sat 🚌 11 Magazine at Octavia St

Rocks Off RPM (3, E5) Come here for that Clash T-shirt you always wanted and pick up the CD while you're at it. This little store has a cool collection of CDs, vinyl and vintage rock 'n' roll wear. ☎ 895-9513 ✉ 4739 Magazine St ⊙ noon-7pm Mon-Sat, noon-5pm Sun 🚌 11 Magazine at Bordeaux St

Bookworm Choices
Want to become a dime-store historian? Peruse some of these titles on your next bookstore visit.
- *Old New Orleans* by Stanley Clisby Arthur details French Quarter architecture and history.
- *The Free People of Color of New Orleans* by Mary Gehman gives an overview of black Creole culture.
- *Mardi Gras Indian* by Michael P Smith peers inside this African-American Mardi Gras tradition.
- *Frenchmen, Desire, Good Children & Other Streets of New Orleans* by cartoonist John Churchill Chase explores the city's history through street names.
- *Literary New Orleans* edited by Richard S Kennedy is a series of essays on famous New Orleans writers and their relationship with the city.
- A classic, *The French Quarter: An Informal History of the New Orleans Underworld* by Herbert Asbury looks at the stories of Storyville, home of whores, birthplace of jazz and final resting place of many.
- Robert Florence's *New Orleans Cemeteries: Life in the Cities of the Dead* is a beautifully illustrated odyssey through the city's unique culture of laying loved ones to rest.

SPECIALIST SHOPS

Aidan Gill for Men (3, J4)
This swank lower Magazine St shop has recreated the era of the old-style barbershop, when the shaves were close, the snifters were strong and the haircuts were precise. Supplies for the gentleman's toilet are also sold.
☎ 587-9090 ✉ 2026 Magazine St ☽ 10am-6pm Tue-Fri, 9am-5pm Sat ☒ 11 Magazine at Sophie Wright Pl

Civil War Store (6, C5)
This pistol-sized store specializes in Confederate memorabilia from guns to bonds and stamps. It also has a few WWII artifacts.
☎ 522-3328 ✉ 212 Chartres St ☽ 10:30am-5:30pm Mon-Sat

Hové Parfumeur (6, D4)
Grassy vetiver, bittersweet orange blossoms, spicy ginger – New Orleans' exotic flora has graciously lent its scents to Hové's house-made perfumes for over 70 years. A brief sniffing visit will leave your head swirling with images of the Vieux Carré's magnificent past. You can ask staff to custom mix a fragrance for you.
☎ 525-7827 ✉ 824 Royal St ☽ 10am-5pm Mon-Sat

James H Cohen & Sons (6, C5) Looking to replace your mother-of-pearl opera glasses? Or complete your collection of Confederate coins? For the serious collector or the serious gawker, this family-owned store is a quirky but fascinating browse.
☎ 522-3305 ✉ 437 Royal St ☽ 9:30am-5:30pm

Little Shop of Fantasy (6, D5) These elaborate handmade masks are crafted out of papier-mâché, leather or cloth, and covered with feathers and jewels. Some evoke medieval European masking traditions, while others look exactly like Michael Jackson.
☎ 529-4243 ✉ 517 St Louis St ☽ 11am-6pm Mon-Sat, 1-6pm Sun

Maskarade (6, D4)
Masks from around the world congregate here to hide the faces of local and visiting revelers. The handmade samples from Africa and Venice are amazing and add to the overall New Orleans mélange. Maskarade offers mask-related gifts as well. How about a demon for your cubicle at work?
☎ 568-0158 ✉ 630 St Ann St ☽ 10am-6pm

Uptown Costume & Dancewear (3, E5) Looking for something suitably shocking for Halloween, Mardi Gras or your sister's wedding? This shop will set you up as everything from Elvis to a survivor of *Plan 9 from Outer Space*. The Dorothy ruby-red sparkling slippers are a steal at $41.
☎ 895-7969 ✉ 4326 Magazine St ☽ 10am-6pm Mon-Fri, 10am-5pm Sat ☒ 11 Magazine at Napoleon Ave

Zombie's House of Voodoo (6, C4) Less crowded than its Bourbon St sister outlet, this store sells a variety of charms and grisgris, from stone arrowheads to correct a bad sense of direction, to the perennial favorite, Love Potion No 9. Zombie's also has a large selection of voodoo statues, including one of Marie Laveau. If you can bear the truth of the tarot cards, have a reading. Depending on the results, you may wish to light up one of their cigars.
☎ 486-6366 ✉ 723 St Peter St ☽ 10am-11pm

Wig out at Uptown Costume & Dancewear

Eating

Eating in New Orleans is part of the fantasy and definitely part of the passion. You'll find foods unlike those anyplace else, in flavors, combinations and just sheer quantity that will amaze. Fortunately for visitors, the locals approach eating with a fervor that is almost out of step with the pervading nonchalance. This guarantees quality and gives you a chance to join the many joyous debates. It won't take long before you're pontificating about who has the best barbecue or gumbo, which new chef is a star and what classic restaurant still shines brightest.

Meal Costs

The pricing symbols used in this chapter indicate the cost for one person for a two-course meal, excluding drinks.

$	under $15
$$	$16–25
$$$	$26–50
$$$$	over $50

Sweet tooth heaven, waistline hell

You can easily put most of the restaurants into three categories: old line, nouvelle and neighborhood. For many, the old-line classics, such as Galatoire's, Antoine's and Commander's Palace, best symbolize the city. At these storied institutions you will enjoy menus handed down for generations. Here you can experience the formal side of Creole culture, with waiters almost as old as the menus presiding over meals that can stretch across hours and a multitude of courses. Your dress will be expected to match the refined air.

Thanks to the fame of celebrity chefs such as Emeril Lagasse and Paul Prudhomme, New Orleans' nouvelle restaurants have almost eclipsed the old-line restaurants in fame, if not fortune. At their restaurants, and scores of others run by chefs who haven't yet made the tube, expect surprising blends of Creole, Cajun and other flavors from around the globe. The menus – like the chef's inspirations – are ever-changing.

The neighborhood joints are where you can really experience and savor eating in New Orleans. Locals are uncompromising when it comes to their meals and what these places lack in pretense they make up for in the intensity of their food. Many are neighborhood cathedrals with devoted followers and charismatic chef-owners who perform culinary miracles day in, day out. (These restaurants are classified as 'New Orleans' in this book.)

If possible, make reservations as far ahead as possible – ideally before you leave home for the most popular places. Otherwise – and this is highly likely at unreservable neighborhood joints – expect a long wait for a table; time you can cheerfully fill with a drink or three and a chat with your brethren about your new favorite places.

FRENCH QUARTER

Acme Oyster House (6, C5) $
Seafood
These bad mother-shuckers might crack open 4000 to 5000 oysters a night. All you have to do is sidle up to the bar, order a dozen and knock 'em back. Sit-down diners will find a long list of other shelled treats including a superb oyster po'boy.
☎ 522-5973 🖳 www .acmeoyster.com ✉ 724 Iberville St 🕙 11am-10pm 🚻

Antoine's (6, C5) $$$
Creole
This restaurant, dating from 1840 and run by a fifth-generation family, is part of New Orleans' dining nobility. Antoine's offers a remarkable time capsule of 19th-century tastes: dishes like *champignons sur tost* and *filet de tuite amandine* are menu stalwarts. Place yourself in the hands of the waiter to navigate the French menu. Jackets required; reservations recommended.
☎ 581-4422 🖳 www .antonies.com ✉ 713-717 St Louis St 🕙 11:30am-2pm, 5:30-9:30pm Mon-Sat

Arnaud's Restaurant (6, C5) $$$
Creole
Another one of the old-time classics; sample oysters Bienville – an original with shrimp, mushrooms, green onions and spices – and other Creole dishes in the elegant dining room (jacket required). The Richelieu

Room, where an acoustic jazz ensemble plays, is less formal (business casual).
☎ 523-5433 🖳 www .arnauds.com ✉ 813 Bienville St 🕙 11:30am-2:30pm, 6-10pm Mon-Fri, 6-10:30pm Sat, 10am-3:30pm, 6-10pm Sun

Brennan's New Orleans (6, C5) $$$
Creole
Brennan's famous breakfast/brunch gives anyone good reason to put a morning cocktail on the menu. Ramos gin fizz and milk punch 'eye openers' help stimulate the appetite for eggs Hussarde and omelette Florentine. Few leave at any time without somehow finding a spot for the famous bananas Foster. Reservations required; ask for the upstairs balcony.
☎ 525-9711 🖳 www .brennansneworleans.com ✉ 417 Royal St 🕙 8am-2:30pm, 6-10pm

Café Beignet (6, C5) $
Café/Breakfast
Not to be confused with Café du Monde, this quaint nook has a lovely shaded patio and serves omelettes, along with other fine breakfast

fare and deli sandwiches.
☎ 522-6868 🖳 www .cafebeignet.com ✉ 334b Royal St 🕙 7am-5pm Ⓥ

Café du Monde (6, D4) $
Café
You won't have to deliberate over a long menu at this classic. The choices are easy: beignets and café au lait. Beignets are square pieces of dough, deep fried and dusted with powdered sugar. Sit outside and watch the passing parade.
☎ 525-4544 🖳 www .cafedumonde.com ✉ 800 Decatur St 🕙 24hr 🚻

Café Sbisa (6, D4) $$$
Creole
Cafe Sbisa has the glamour of a Hollywood grande dame – a little flash and a lot of grace. The patio overlooks Decatur St, while the indoor dining room has a view of the mural over the bar. The Sunday jazz brunch is also a crowd pleaser.
☎ 522-5565 🖳 www .cafesbisa.com ✉ 1011 Decatur St 🕙 5:30-10:30pm Sun-Thu, 5:30-11pm Fri & Sat, brunch 10:30am-3pm Sun Ⓥ

Light My Fire
Some parts of the country invent superconductors, electric light bulbs, or other useless crap, while New Orleans invents food. Bananas Foster, a classic American dessert, was born at Brennan's Restaurant in 1951. The pyromaniacal chef sliced a few bananas, sauteed them in butter, brown sugar, cinnamon and liqueur, and then set the whole mess ablaze with some rum. Folks are suckers for fiery dishes.

Alfresco dining at the Court of Two Sisters

Central Grocery
(6, D4) $
Deli
The muffuletta was born in 1906 at this busy grocery and deli, at the hands of the Sicilian owner, Salvatore Lupo. This famous sandwich combines ham, salami, provolone and olive relish between slices of flat, round and crispy muffuletta bread. Counter service is quick and you can gobble down your delight at a stool or on a bench along the Mississippi.
☎ 523-1620 ✉ 923 Decatur St ⏱ 8am-5:30pm Mon-Sat, 9am-5:30pm Sun ♿

Clover Grill (6, D4) $
Diner
Want a little 'shake' with those fries? Dancing waiters and pulsating techno heats up the Clover Grill, a diner that rocks with the beat of nearby Bourbon St clubs. The burgers are good too.
☎ 598-1010 🖳 www.clovergrill.com ✉ 900 Bourbon St ⏱ 24hr

Coop's Place (6, E4) $
New Orleans/Bar
More bar than restaurant, Coop's makes one of the best gumbos in the Quarter and is a sure bet for a relaxed, need-to-feed experience. Hungry hordes

descend for late meals, both sublime and surreal.
☎ 525-9053 ✉ 1109 Decatur St ⏱ 11am-2am

Court of Two Sisters
(6, C5) $$$
Creole
If you want to try all of New Orleans' signature dishes, then come here for the daily jazz brunch. Sample over 80 dishes, from boiled crawfish to shrimp *rémoulade*, on the pleasant wisteria-shaded patio. Nothing's a standout but you'll leave sated and smiling.
☎ 522-7261 🖳 www.courtoftwosisters.com ✉ 613 Royal St ⏱ 9am-3pm, 5:30-10pm ♿

Croissant d'Or Patisserie
(6, D4) $
Café/Bakery
Behind the scenes at this beautifully tiled bakery, toqued chefs are hard at work making fresh croissants and French pastries. The coffee is as thick as molasses and contrasts nicely with this quiet patch of the Quarter.
☎ 524-4663 ✉ 615-617 Ursulines Ave
⏱ 7am-5pm

Evelyn's Place
(6, C5) $
New Orleans/Deli & Bar
Evelyn's doesn't see much

action until late at night. During the day, you've got the place to yourself for a meal of red beans and rice, an Abita from the tap and room to contemplate.
☎ 522-2216 ✉ 139 Chartres St ⏱ 11am-late

Fiorella's
(6, E4) $
New Orleans
Informality draws locals to Fiorella's, where just about anything (crispy chicken, pickles, savory pies) is fried. Salads serve those looking beyond meat and hot oil.
☎ 528-9566 ✉ 45 French Market Pl
⏱ 7am-midnight Sun-Thu, to 2am Fri & Sat ♿ Ⓥ

Galatoire's
(6, C5) $$$
Creole
Of the old-liners, Galatoire's gets the most compliments for its seafood dishes. A hidden highlight is Galatoire's fried eggplant (dipped in powdered sugar). If you've been wondering where to order oysters Florentine, do so here. Reservations required for upstairs, and it's first come, first served for downstairs; jackets required. Waiters rule the roost and hold star status.
☎ 525-2021 ✉ 209 Bourbon St ⏱ 11:30am-10pm Tue-Sat, noon-10:30pm Sun

Irene's Cuisine
(6, D4) $$
Italian
The flavors of New Orleans and Sicily are wed amid the romantic environs of this

family-owned eatery. Specialties include oysters Irene, duck St Philip and soft-shell crab. Many consider this their 'hidden' Quarter find. No reservations.
☎ 529-8811 ✉ 539 St Philip St ⏲ 5:30-10:30pm Sun-Thu, 5:30-11pm Fri & Sat

Johnny's Po'Boys (6, D5) $
New Orleans
Well-worn, Johnny's delivers superb stuffed po'boys. The fried oyster number (lightly breaded in cornmeal) will turn a raw oyster purist into a devotee. Chow down by the river or on a cruise on the *Natchez* (p39).
☎ 524-8129 ✉ 511 St Louis St ⏲ 8am-4:30pm Mon-Fri, 9am-4pm Sat & Sun ⏲

K-Paul's Louisiana Kitchen (6, C5) $$$
Contemporary Cajun
After almost three decades, chef Paul Prudhomme's signature eatery is still great. Favorites include blackened twin beef tenders with debris (gravy) sauce, and amazing jambalaya. Reservations required for upstairs; first come, first served for downstairs; business casual. The service here is tops.
☎ 524-7394 🖳 www .kpauls.com ✉ 416 Chartres St ⏲ 11:30am-2:30pm Thu-Sat, 5:30-10pm Mon-Sat

Lulu's (6, C5) $$
Californian
Simple and fresh salads, hearty sandwiches and intoxicating desserts head the lunchtime lineup in

Try the blackened treats at K-Paul's Louisiana Kitchen

a space no bigger than a closet and less formal than the corner grocery. It's also worth venturing down the alley for dinner, when the more complex menu reflects what's fresh.
☎ 525-2600 ✉ 307 Exchange Alley ⏲ 10:30am-3pm Mon-Sat, 6-9:30pm Thu-Sat V

Mona Lisa Restaurant (6, D3) $
Pizzeria
This neighborhood pizza joint offers a safe haven from the crowds and fuss of the Quarter. With knockoff

paintings of the famous old broad and soft lighting, Mona Lisa offers a dose of atmosphere to go with the excellent pizza.
☎ 522-6746 ✉ 1212 Royal St ⏲ 11am-11pm ⏲ V

Napoleon House (6, C5) $
New Orleans
In the 1820s, New Orleanians cooked up a plan to liberate Napoleon from exile and transplant him to this house. The story lived longer than the plan, or the emperor for that matter, and adds a dash of fame to

Best Dressed
Po'boys are New Orleans' version of the submarine sandwich. A crusty French bread loaf is hollowed out and stuffed with just about anything: fried oysters, traditional lunch meats, French fries or all of the above. Po'boy is a shortened version of 'poor boy,' a name earned during the Depression, when the sandwiches cost only a quarter. The po'boy comes in whole and half sizes, either of which can feed a hungry brass band. Ask for it 'dressed' to get lettuce, tomato and mayo. Five excellent choices for po'boys: **Johnny's Po'Boys** (above), **Mother's Restaurant** (p55), **Parasol's Restaurant & Bar** (p58) **Domilise's Po-Boys** (p57) and **Liuzza's by the Track** (p59).

a great bar. The food menu is classic New Orleans – the muffulettas are good – and can be enjoyed in a candlelit courtyard.

☎ 524-9752 ▢ www .napoleonhouse.com ✉ 500 Chartres St ◷ 11am-midnight Mon-Thu, 11am-1am Fri & Sat, 11am-7pm Sun 🚹

NOLA (6, C5) $$$
Louisiana Contemporary
All of Emeril's personality is on display at this larger-than-life Quarter hotspot that thrills throngs daily. Boldly spiced Cajun and Creole dishes enjoy new interpretations. Desserts are a must, no matter what common sense says. Grab one of the counter seats overlooking the kitchen if you're dining solo and

Over easy, Clover Grill (p50)

Save the Vegetables

Thanks to New Orleans' proximity to bodies of water, vegetarians who eat fish will have an easy culinary trip. For the vegetable-lover or stricter vegetarian, the road will be pretty rocky. New Orleanians consider the only good vegetable to be a fried one.

Unassuming **Lulu's** (p51) is a little piece of California's whole-food scene in the French Quarter. Over in Marigny, **Marisol** (right) always has several good options. Organic and vegetarian grocery items can be collected at **Whole Foods Market** (4, C4; ☎ 943-1626; 3135 Esplanade Ave), in Esplanade Ridge. For locally grown veggies, boiled peanuts and local color, head to the **Crescent City Farmer's Market** (p45).

want some fun. Reservations are essential.

☎ 522-6652 ▢ www .emerils.com ✉ 534 St Louis St ◷ 6-10:30pm Sun, 11:30am-2pm, 6-10:30pm Mon-Thu, 11:30am-2pm, 6-11pm Fri & Sat

Olivier's (6, C6) $$
Creole
Without all the decorum of the old-line restaurants, Olivier's stays true to the Creole commandments while satisfying modern palates. Inheriting recipes from five generations, this family-owned restaurant serves up the kind of classic, comfort fare you'd expect from a Creole mom. Gumbo comes in many forms.

☎ 525-7734 ✉ 204 Decatur St ◷ 11am-3pm, 5-10pm Ⓥ

Stella! (6, D4) $$$
Louisiana Contemporary
The name is a riff on the Marlon Brando movie, but the shouting ends at the door at this refined little

spot in a quiet corner of the Quarter. Local ingredients join forces with other American classics to create a changing fusion menu that's grounded locally. Service is gracious and you can expect an elegant evening. Smart-casual dress is preferred.

☎ 587-0091 ▢ www .hotelprovincial.com ✉ Hotel Provincial, 1032 Chartres St ◷ 5:30-10pm Mon, Wed & Thu, 5:30-10:30pm Sat & Sun

Tujague's (6, D4) $$
Creole
Crisp white tablecloths, a checkered-tiled floor and a commanding cypress bar create an alluring Old-World ambience that's little changed since it opened in 1856. Tujague's (Two-Jacks) offers a five-course set menu, including a beef brisket locals salivate over; reservations recommended.

☎ 525-8676 ▢ www .tujagues.com ✉ 823 Decatur St ◷ 11am-3pm, 5-11pm

FAUBOURG MARIGNY & BYWATER

Elizabeth's
(2, E2) $
New Orleans

Elizabeth's hearty sandwiches and down-home breakfasts deliver on the rumor that good food lies ahead. The endangered Creole breakfast dish called *calas* – deep-fried rice balls dusted in powdered sugar – can be ordered here. Either way, make sure you have the praline bacon on your plate.

☎ 944-9272 ▫ www .elizabeths-restaurant .com ✉ 601 Gallier St ◷ 7am-2:30pm Tue-Sat, open some Sun ⊖ cab or drive ⟆

Flora's Café
(6, F3) $
Café

This neighborhood coffee shop serves as an informal civic center for the many artisan residents of Marigny and Bywater. Poetry readings on Monday nights, local art displays and veggie burritos join the cast of regulars.

☎ 947-8358 ✉ 2600 **Royal St at Franklin Ave** ◷ 8am-midnight ⊟ 5 Marigny/Bywater at Franklin ⟆ Ⓥ

La Peniche (6, E3) $
New Orleans

All sorts of night owls make this Faubourg Marigny corner joint a character study in eccentricity. Reliable local standards are joined by tasty breakfasts and good late-night desserts. The engaging staff are unflappable.

☎ 943-1460 ✉ 1940 **Dauphine St** ◷ 24hr Thu-Tue

Marisol
(6, E4) $$$
Contemporary Louisiana

Marisol is the brainchild of Peter Vazquez, whose menu changes nightly and reflects what's fresh, along with the whim of the moment. Consider these choices: potato-crusted atlantic skate 'holstein' with squid ink spaetzle, and grilled pork porterhouse with rock shrimp, Manchego cheese stuffing, arbol chili sauce and a mango, jicama and avocado salad. Make certain you have a table in the romantic garden.

☎ 943-1912 ▫ www .marisolrestaurant.com ✉ 437 Esplanade Ave ◷ 11am-2pm, 6-10pm Wed, Thu & Sun, 11am-2pm, 6-11pm Fri & Sat Ⓥ

Late-Night Eats

For late-night sustenance, follow Bourbon St past the strip clubs and bead shops to **Clover Grill** (p50), where a diner-sized disco sizzles in the wee hours. **La Peniche** (above) in Marigny, **Huey's 24/7 Diner** (p54) in the CBD and **Camellia Grill** (p56), in Riverbend, are other good options for late-night comfort fare.

Coop's Place (p50), in the Quarter, serves classic Creole until 3am and **Cooter Brown's Tavern & Oyster Bar** (p56), in Riverbend, has a long Cajun menu most nights until after 3am. The advantage here is that the bar stays open even longer.

Yee-haw, pah-ner! Head on down to Cooter Brown's (p56) for a late-night feed

CBD & WAREHOUSE DISTRICT

Bon Ton Café
(5, E3) $$
Cajun
Crawfish and crisp napkins are the recipes for success at this dignified old restaurant. Servers lavish attention and the iced tea refills arrive only slightly more often than more bread. Crawfish appear on the menu more than a dozen times and seem to be most of the specials as well. That's just as well. They're good.
☎ 524-3386 ✉ 401 Magazine St ⏱ 11am-2pm, 5-9:30pm

Cuvée
(5, E3) $$$
Louisiana Contemporary
Classy Cuvée introduces Creole to other regional and international cuisines. Sugarcane-smoked duck breast with seared Hudson Valley foie gras and pear glacé could follow a prelude of spiced shrimp and crisp mirliton with classic *rémoulade*. The wine list wins raves. Reservations recommended; business casual.
☎ 587-9001 ⌨ www.restaurantcuvee.com ✉ 322 Magazine St ⏱ 11:30am-2:30pm, 6-10pm Mon-Thu, 11:30am-2:30pm, 6-11pm Fri, 6-11pm Sat 🚌 11 Magazine at Gravier St

Emeril's
(5, E4) $$$
Louisiana Contemporary
Emeril Lagasse is easily the most famous chef in America, but while overexposure is always a concern, the food here is redolent with all the 'bam!' style of seasoning one would expect. The eclectic menu jumps from Creole sauces to Italian raviolis to straight-shooting Americana. Reservations required; business casual.
☎ 528-9393 ⌨ www.emerils.com ✉ 800 Tchoupitoulas St ⏱ 11:30am-2pm Mon-Fri, 6-10pm Sun-Thu, 6-11pm Fri & Sat 🚌 10 Tchoupitoulas at Julia St

Herbsaint
(5, D4) $$
Louisiana Contemporary
Named after the local anise liqueur, Herbsaint reflects the combined talents of noted local chef Susan Spicer and protégé Donald Link. The menu is a mix of trad New Orleans, Mediterranean and nouvelle and the results have bold flavors. Many dishes can be ordered on small plates for grazing joy. Dinner reservations recommended; business casual.
☎ 524-4114 ✉ 701 St Charles Ave ⏱ 11:30am-2pm, 5-10pm Mon-Thu, 11:30am-2pm, 5-11pm Fri, 5-11pm Sat 🚃 St Charles at Girod St

Huey's 24/7 Diner
(5, E3) $
Diner
Ready for some upscale breakfast chow after a night at the bars? At Huey's you can have some top-notch fare and let the night roll on as the bar here never closes. Less boozy options include malts, which go down

Business Dining
You'll not be likely to conduct business in the French Quarter (unless it's monkey business…), so taking those important associates out for a meal will have to happen elsewhere. Three good choices are not far from most hotels: **August** (right) in the CBD, **Herbsaint** (above) in the Warehouse District, and **Emeril's Delmonico** (p57) in the Lower Garden District. All three have smooth professional service, quiet ambience and well-spaced tables.

Skip mains and go straight for dessert at Praline Connection

well with the piled-high sandwiches.

☎ 598-4839 ✉ 200 Magazine St ⏲ 24hr

Mother's Restaurant (5, E3) $

New Orleans

Mother's Is New Orleans Cuisine 101 to scores of happy diners daily. It's packed, there's a long line, a chaotic ordering system and incredible specialties, such as the roast beef and debris po'boy. When they have their home-baked ham, order it. Get some jambalaya too.

☎ 523-9656
✉ 401 Poydras St
⏲ 7am-10pm ♿

Praline Connection (5, E5) $$

New Orleans/Soul

Two blocks from the convention center, Praline Connection stirs the soul with stuffed crab, fried chicken, red beans and rice, and a two-seating Sunday gospel brunch. A praline candy shop and second location on Frenchmen St (No 542; ☎ 943-3934) testify to the restaurant's success.

☎ 523-3973 🖥 www .pralineconnection .com ✉ 907 S Peters St ⏲ 11am-3pm Mon-Fri, 11am-1pm & 2-4pm Sun 🚌 10 Tchoupitoulas at St Joseph St ♿

Restaurant August (5, E3) $$$

Louisiana Contemporary

French cuisine gets a New Orleans and nouvelle overlay at this superb restaurant headed by John Besh. Set in an old tobacco warehouse,

this refined place has a changing seasonal menu, but look for exquisite spiced duck, innovative Gulf seafood and desserts that always excel.

☎ 299-9777 🖥 www .rest-august.com ✉ 301 Tchoupitoulas St ⏲ 11am-2pm, 5:30-10pm Mon-Fri, 5:30-10pm Sat

RioMar (5, E5) $$

Spanish/Mediterranean

Two blocks from the convention center, this seafood restaurant features dishes from Spain and its former colonies. RioMar's ceviches amaze New Orleanians who don't know that fish aren't born deep fried. Reservations recommended; business casual.

☎ 525-3474 ✉ 800 S Peters St ⏲ 11:30am-2pm, 6-10pm Mon-Thu, 11:30am-2pm, 6-11pm Fri, 6-11pm Sat 🚊 Riverfront at Julia St Ⓥ

Tommy's (5, E4) $$

Italian-Creole

Garlic wafts through the

Pralines: sugar for the soul

rafters at this refined and inviting Warehouse District newcomer. The pasta dishes gain the zest of local seasonings and the Gulf supplies excellent seafood. Service is smooth and friendly at once, making you feel like a regular from your first visit.

☎ 581-1103, ✉ 746 Tchoupitoulas St ⏲ 5:30-10:30pm Sun-Thu, 5:30-11pm Fri & Sat 🚌 10 Tchoupitoulas at Julia St

Death on a Bun

It had to happen. In a town where everything from pickles to bananas to every form of meat gets tossed in the deep fryer, it was just a matter of time before cheeseburgers joined the pack. At **Tucker's Tavern** (5, A2; ☎ 522-0440; 635 S Roman St) in the shadow of both the Superdome and (fittingly) a major hospital, you can get a stuffed and deep-fried burger. A ½lb burger is stuffed with various cardiac-arresting ingredients (cheese, bacon, sausage et al), battered and deep-fried. The result defies description and good health, but it is amazingly moist and juicy.

GARDEN DISTRICTS, UPTOWN & RIVERBEND

Bluebird Café
(3, F4) $
Breakfast
Start your morning the way God intended with pancakes or Belgian-style waffles in dizzying varieties: traditional, buckwheat, butter pecan, banana, blueberry and silver dollar. Or try the killer *huevos rancheros*. Lines can be long. Cash only.
☎ 895-7166 ✉ 3625 Prytania St 🕐 7am-3pm Mon-Fri, 8am-3pm Sat & Sun 🚋 St Charles at Amelia St ♿

Brigtsen's Restaurant
(3, A2) $$
Creole
In this romantic little house, chef Frank Brigtsen puts a fresh spin on local ingredients. His deft hand in the kitchen has brought him accolades from afar. The changing menu is broadranging. Whatever you do, save room for the banana bread pudding.
☎ 861-7610 🖥 www .brigtsen.com ✉ 723 Dante St 🕐 5:30-10pm

Tue-Sat 🚋 St Charles at Maple St

Camellia Grill
(3, A2) $
Diner
Only in New Orleans would a greasy spoon come packaged in a Greek Revival mini-mansion. Camellia Grill serves diner favorites (the burgers are amazing), as well as signature milkshakes and chocolate pecan pies. Cash only.
☎ 866-9573 ✉ 626 S Carrollton Ave 🕐 9am-1am Mon-Thu, 9am-3am Fri, 8am-3am Sat, 8am-1am Sun 🚋 St Charles at S Carrollton Ave ♿

Casamento's
(3, E5) $
New Orleans
Since 1949 this oyster institution has figured prominently in many families' dining routines. In this gleaming interior, you'll wonder if you've gone to 'raw bar' heaven. Cash only.
☎ 895-9761 ✉ 4330 Magazine St

🕐 11:30am-1:30pm, 5:30-9pm Tue-Sun, closed summer 🚌 11 Magazine at Napoleon Ave ♿

Commander's Palace
(3, G4) $$$$
Creole
Neatly coiffed ladies in their Sunday best file into this Garden District old-liner dating from the 1880s, but they don't have the joint to themselves: Commander's is regularly voted New Orleans' most popular restaurant. Reservations required; try for the upstairs parlor or Garden Room; jackets required.
☎ 899-8221 🖥 www .commanderspalace.com ✉ 1403 Washington Ave 🕐 11:30am-2pm, 6-10pm Mon-Fri, 11:30am-1pm, 6-10pm Sat, 10:30am-1:30pm, 6-10pm Sun 🚋 St Charles at Washington Ave

Cooter Brown's Tavern & Oyster Bar
(3, A2) $
Bar & Grill
Raw oysters, damn good po'boys, superb onion rings and a four-page beer menu – yee-haw, pah-ner! You should plan on staying a while if you make the trek to this Riverbend dive where the bar is open later than the food hours listed below.
☎ 866-9104 🖥 www .cooterbrowns.com ✉ 509 S Carrollton Ave 🕐 11am-3am Mon-Thu, 11am-4am Fri, 11am-2am Sun 🚋 St Charles at S Carrollton Ave

---

Oyster Cult

Baked, grilled, raw, deep fried, thrown in gumbo, made into soup – New Orleans has found 1001 delicious recipes for these mollusks.

Old-line restaurants always have a house baked-oyster dish. The most recognized nationally is Antoine's oysters Rockefeller; the rich sauce (hence the John D connection) is made of spinach, breadcrumbs, bacon, spices and anise liqueur spooned over the half-shelled oysters before baking. Equally addictive are oysters on the half shell. Raw bars in New Orleans are as revered as old-line restaurants, but are a lot more fun.

**Dante's Kitchen
(3, A1)** $$
Louisiana Contemporary
Steps from the Mississippi, in a cozy 1860s cottage, Dante's creates honest food, such as grilled shrimp BLT sandwiches, seared grouper and sweet potato pie. They even have a wild boar cookout. Enjoy a Sunday brunch on the garden patio; dinner reservations required.
☎ 861-3121 ▯ www .danteskitchen.com ✉ 736 Dante St ◔ 11:30am-2:30pm, 5:30-10pm ▭ St Charles at Maple St

**Dick & Jenny's
(3, E6)** $$
Creole
Another Uptown place that scores with locals, who part the shading palms to dine in this no-fuss little cottage. The Creole food is standout; try the crawfish cheesecake, fried oysters and the fried green tomatoes with crab cakes. Can't decide on a starter? Have them all with the sampler.
☎ 894-9880 ✉ 4501 Tchoupitoulas St ◔ 5:30-10pm Tue-Sat ▭ 10 Tchoupitoulas at Jena St

**Domilise's Po-Boys
(3, D6)** $
New Orleans
It's a mouthful, but locals swear by the hot smoked sausage po'boy with chili gravy and Creole mustard. Domilise's is a convivial but otherwise unadorned bar; cash only.
☎ 899-9126 ✉ 5240 Annunciation St ◔ 11am-7pm Mon-Sat ▭ 10 Tchoupitoulas or

Southern Lobster

You've seen his likeness on magnets and aprons, and if your visit is timed just right you can get chummy with Louisiana's unofficial mascot – no, not Emeril – the crawfish. A native swamp dweller, the crawfish is about three inches long and was credited with founding the universe, according to Native American mythology. Since then its accomplishments have been quite small: the crawfish industry generates about $125 million annually and employs roughly 7000 people in the state.

Frozen tail meat is available year-round and is typically used in étouffée, gumbo and the like. However mid-February to June is crawfish season, and the little guys get thrown whole into a pot of boiling water, seasoned with cayenne pepper and other spices until bright red, and then served to a smiling public. See p29 for tips on head sucking.

11 Magazine at Bellecastle St ⬚

Dunbar's (3, D3) $
Soul
Why is Dunbar's popular? It's not the neighborhood, which is way Uptown and on the shaggy side. Oh that's right, it's the all-you-can-eat red beans and rice and fried-chicken lunch special. See ya there, the food's amazing.
☎ 899-0734 ✉ 4927 Freret St ◔ 7am-9pm Mon-Sat ▭ cab or drive

**Emeril's Delmonico
(3, J2)** $$$$
Creole
This is one refined restaurant. Service is exemplary and from the moment you arrive, your experience will progress from one high to the next. The menu is traditional with the usual bold Emeril flair. Look for classics prepared tableside

such as Caesar salad and bananas Foster. If you don't have a special occasion to come here, invent one.
☎ 525-4937 ▯ www .emerils.com ✉ 1300 St Charles Ave ◔ 10:30am-2pm, 6-10pm Sun, 11:30am-1:30pm, 6-10pm Mon-Thu, 11:30am-1:30pm, 6-11pm Fri, 6-11pm Sat ▭ St Charles at Erato St

**Franky & Johnny's
(3, C6)** $
New Orleans
When it is crawfish season, go straight to this down-home joint and get yourself a platter of the boiled buggers. The picnic tables are covered in red-checked plastic and you'll rub elbows with lots of neighborhood stalwarts.
☎ 899-9146 ✉ 321 Arabella St ◔ 11am-10pm ▭ 10 Tchoupitoulas at Arabella ⬚

Jacques-Imos (3, A1) $$
Creole/Southern
This casual joint is so popular with locals that they'll gladly drink away a few hours waiting for a table. Shrimp and alligator sausage cheesecake, calamari, crawfish étouffée and fried chicken top the greatest-hits list. Chef Jacques Leonardi has staked his claim for title of best casual place for New Orleans chow.
☎ 861-0886 ✉ 8324 Oak St ⏰ 5:30-10pm Mon-Thu, 5:30-10:30pm Fri & Sat 🚋 St Charles at Oak St

Lilette (3, F5) $$$
French
Chef John Harris has created an Uptown gem. The ever-changing bistro menu is creative and assertive at the same time, with French classics coming in for some deft Creole treatment. The main dining room is done up in creamy leather and looks onto Magazine St. Avoid the unpopular back room.
☎ 895-1636 ✉ 3637 Magazine St ⏰ 11:30am-2pm, 6-10pm Tue-Thu, 11:30am-2pm, 6-11pm Fri & Sat 🚌 11 Magazine at Antonine St

Parasol's Restaurant & Bar (3, H4) $
New Orleans/Bar
Does Parasol's serve the best roast beef po'boy on the planet? Certainly any research on the topic must take in this neighborhood bar near Magazine St. The St Patrick's Day celebrations here rival Mardi Gras.
☎ 899-2054 ✉ 2533 Constance St ⏰ 11am-10pm 🚋 St Charles at Third St

Pascal's Manale (3, E4) $$
Creole/Italian
Where's Frank? It's a natural question at this family friendly 1950s supper club, where shots of the stars adorn the walls. The food combines Italian comfort with local excitement. The barbecue shrimp are 'duck and cover' radioactive with pepper and garlic.
☎ 895-4877 ✉ 1838 Napoleon Ave ⏰ 11am-10pm Mon-Sat, 11am-9pm Sun 🚕 cab or drive ♿

Tee-Eva's Creole Soul Food (3, E5) $
Creole/Soul
Place your order at the window of this squat yellow building and you'll be rewarded with an amazing plate of sausage jambalaya, or seafood gumbo. Before heading to the nearby park to eat, grab a sweet potato pie or praline. Or try a local favorite, a sno ball (shaved ice flavored with syrup).
☎ 899-8350 ✉ 4430 Magazine St ⏰ 11am-7pm 🚌 11 Magazine at Napoleon Ave ♿

Uglesich's (3, H2) $
Seafood
Two blocks off St Charles Ave in an unadorned building, this is the lunch joint you've heard about. Renowned for seafood of all kinds, Uglesich's flexes its muscles in the fresh-catch department; ask for recommendations. The shrimp Uggie is a spicy miracle. The early bird gets a table, or at least a wait by the 'raw bar.' Cash only; reservations not accepted.
☎ 523-8571 ✉ 1238 Baronne St ⏰ 11am-2pm Mon-Fri 🚋 St Charles at Erato St

Upperline Restaurant (3, D5) $$$
Louisiana Contemporary
Owner JoAnn Clevenger has created one of the city's best restaurants. It's both unassuming and exquisitely refined. Fine art contrasts with a relaxing vibe and the food is simply great. Try their famous fried green tomatoes in a shrimp rémoulade. Reservations required.
☎ 891-9822 🖥 www .upperline.com ✉ 1413 Upperline St ⏰ 5:30-10pm Wed-Sun 🚋 St Charles at Upperline St

See food, eat food, enjoy food at Uglesich

MID-CITY, FAIR GROUNDS & CITY PARK

Café Degas
(4, C4) $$
French
This charming café serves Parisian-style fare such as quiches, salad Niçoise and a mean beef tenderloin with blue-cheese butter. This is a very cosmopolitan finish to a day at nearby New Orleans Museum of Art. Go for the tables outside.
☎ 945-5635 🖳 www .cafedegas.com
✉ 3127 Esplanade Ave
🕑 5:30-10pm Mon, 11:30am-2:30pm, 5:30-10pm Tue-Thu, 11:30am-2:30pm, 6-10:30pm Fri, 11:30am-3pm, 6-10:30pm Sat, 10:30am-3:30pm, 6-10pm Sun 🚌 48 Esplanade at Ponce de Leon St 🚹

Dooky Chase Restaurant
(4, C5) $$
Soul/Creole
Ray Charles sang about it, Sarah Vaughan liked the soft-shell crab, and Lena Horne favored the fried chicken. A lot of famous African-Americans have come through Dooky's door, especially when they were barred. Today, everyone comes because Leah Chase puts the kind of love you can taste into her Southern and Creole dishes.
☎ 821-0600 ✉ 2301 Orleans Ave 🕑 11:30am-10pm Sun-Thu, 11:30am-midnight Fri & Sat 🚗 cab or drive only

Gabrielle (4, C4) $$$
Louisiana Contemporary
This small operation looks barebones from the outside

Garden Dining
Sitting outside savoring a sensational meal on a sultry night is one of New Orleans' great pleasures. The following three places have gardens you won't want to leave: **Stella!** (p520) in the Quarter, **Marisol** (p53) in nearby Marigny and **Commander's Palace** (p56) in the Garden District.

---

but is as romantic as heck inside. Oysters Gabi (with artichokes, pancetta, spices and Parmesan) and mojo-marinated pork chops are exciting twists on the norm. Don't forget the dessert.
☎ 948-6233 ✉ 3201 Esplanade Ave 🕑 5:30-10pm Tue-Sat, 11:30am-2pm Fri 🚌 48 Esplanade at Ponce de Leon St

Indigo (4, C5) $$$
Creole
A stunning plantation-style dining room accented with garden-motif brass work is ensconced in a 1798 plantation house. The food is as refined as you'd expect. Menus change often but always reflect the ingredients of the season. Preparations lean to Mediterranean, with lighter sauces supplanting Creole standards. Reservations required; business casual.

☎ 947-0123 ✉ 2285 Bayou Rd 🕑 5:30-10pm Tue-Sat 🚌 48 Esplanade at Ponce de Leon St

Liuzza's by the Track
(4, C4) $
New Orleans
Inside this simple corner bar is amazing food that wins raves. How about a roast beef po'boy that has meat marinated in garlic and served with horseradish mayo? Or volcanic barbecued shrimp po'boys? Whatever you choose, chase it down with a goblet of beer. Note: in the New Orleans lexicon, barbecued shrimp isn't barbecued but sautéed in butter, garlic and pepper.
☎ 943-8667 ✉ 1518 N Lopez 🕑 11am-8:30pm Mon-Fri, 11am-4:30pm Sat 🚌 48 Esplanade at Ponce de Leon St

If you can't handle the heat, get outta the kitchen

Entertainment

From month-long parties to 24-hour bars, New Orleans loves a good time. It's given birth to a million cocktails, as classy as the Sazerac and as campy as the hurricane. Drinking is such a basic part of the culture that it is perfectly legal to escort a plastic 'go cup' of booze to your next destination.

Visitors stumble most easily into the year-round Mardi Gras on Bourbon St, where beads rain down on proffered parts below. Drink stands, cover-band dance clubs, boozy jazz dives and strip joints are all part of the hustle. Thankfully, the Big Easy has scores of bars elsewhere in the Quarter, and in places like Faubourg Marigny and the neighborhoods along St Charles Ave, where you can find the real soul of the city. Pull up a stool, join the regulars in a joke and let the good times roll.

Mood lighting at a Bourbon St dive bar

Beyond simply getting schnockered, the Crescent City rocks, rumbles and jams to the strains of jazz and R&B. Brass instruments like tubas and trumpets are adored, having never been deposed by rock's electric guitar. And in the simple music clubs, five-piece bands cram onto little stages, with the audience only a trombone's slide away. The closeness creates an instant community demonstrating New Orleans' strongest talent – bringing everyone to the party. Even traditional holidays like Halloween and Christmas are infused with New Orleans' unique party touch.

For listings of upcoming shows, refer to the weekly entertainment newspaper *Gambit* or the *Times-Picayune's* Friday entertainment, 'Lagniappe.'

Since there isn't a city-enforced closing time, bars stay open as long as there are customers; some never close their doors. In New Orleans your nights can easily blur into your days.

Find your rhythm and avoid the blues on Bourbon St

Special Events

January *Sugar Bowl* – on or near Jan 1; two of the nation's top-ranked college football teams spar in the Superdome at the first big party event of the year
Twelfth Night – Jan 6; Carnival season kicks off with costume parties and parades

February *Mardi Gras* – February or early March; Fat Tuesday marks the orgasmic finale of the Carnival season (see p8 for future dates)

March *Black Heritage Festival* (☎ 827-0112) – second weekend; African-American contributions to food and the arts are recognized, with cultural events held citywide
St Patrick's Day – March 17; a day of revelry, especially in the Irish Channel neighborhood near the Garden District; on or near the day a Magazine St parade features floats and throws of potatoes, carrots and the biggest prize, cabbages
Tennessee Williams Literary Festival (🖳 www.tennesseewilliams.net) – end of March; five days of literary events and parties celebrate the playwright's work

April/May *French Quarter Festival* (🖳 www.frenchquarterfestivals.org) – second weekend of April; twelve stages of music, tours and lots of street parties
Jazz Fest – late April or early May; 10 days of music, food, crafts and fun (see p10)
Spring Fiesta (☎ 800-550-8450) – April or May; private historic homes are opened to the public

June *French Market Creole Tomato Festival* (☎ 504-522-2621) second weekend; tastings, demonstrations and more using the first local tomatoes of the season

July *Essence Music Festival* (🖳 www.essence.com) – Independence Day weekend; star-studded performances at the Superdome with additional stages featuring local acts and motivational speakers; the entire event has the feel of a huge reunion

August *Satchmo Fest* (🖳 www.frenchquarterfestivals.org) – August 2–4; music and lectures honor the birthday of New Orleans' favorite son, Louis Armstrong

September *Southern Decadence* – Labor Day weekend; a huge gay, lesbian and transgender festival, including a leather block party (see p68)

October *Art for Arts Sake* (🖳 www.magazinestreet.com, www.cacno.org) – first week; scores of galleries and studios are open in the Warehouse District and along Magazine St; the Contemporary Arts Center throws – you guessed it – a huge party to mark the occasion
Louisiana Swampfest (🖳 www.audoboninstitute.org) – first two weekends; the Audubon Institute (p19) celebrates Cajun food, music, culture and critters

December *Feux de Joie* – December 24; 'fires of joy' light the way along the Mississippi River levees
New Year's Eve – December 31; Baby New Year is dropped from the roof of Jackson Brewery at midnight

BARS & DANCE CLUBS

Bombay Club (6, C5)
Easily the most cultured place for a drink in the Quarter, the Bombay Club is darkly lit with a warm glow coming from the illuminated bottles behind the bar. The bartenders are pros and there's a good wine selection by the glass.
☎ 586-0972 ✉ 830 Conti St 💲 no cover 🕑 5pm-late

Café Brasil (6, E3)
Music and conversation spill out onto the street at this Chartres St club. With a bright breezy attitude, Cafe Brasil peddles itself as 'global human music box' featuring Latin, jazz, reggae and acoustic bands.
☎ 949-0851 ✉ 2100 Chartres St 💲 $5 🕑 6pm-2am Sun-Thu, 6pm-4am Fri & Sat

Carousel Bar (6, C5)
The Carousel Bar, in the Hotel Monteleone, is just that: a complete revolution takes about 15 minutes. The center bar is canopied by the top hat of the 1904 world fair's carousel complete with

Bright, breezy Café Brasil

running lights, hand-painted figures and gilded mirrors. The Vieux Carré, a distant cousin of the Manhattan, is the house cocktail.
☎ 523-3341 ✉ 214 Royal St 💲 no cover 🕑 11am-late

The Columns Hotel (3, F4) This is about as close as you can get in the Crescent City to living the life of an old-South colonel, sitting on the veranda of your mansion. The outdoor tables face a gorgeous stretch of St Charles Ave.
☎ 899-9308 🖥 www .columnshotel.com ✉ 3811 St Charles Ave 💲 no cover 🕑 3pm-midnight 🚋 St Charles at General Taylor St

Cooter Brown's Tavern & Oyster Bar (3, A2) This college-crowd and neighborhood hangout serves over 400 different beers; try the amazing local Abita Purple Haze on tap. Tables out front let you watch passing freight trains. Inside there are huge TVs for sports. The food (p56) is tops.
☎ 866-9104 🖥 www .cooterbrowns.com ✉ 509 S Carrollton Ave 💲 no cover 🕑 11am-very late 🚋 St Charles at S Carrollton Ave

d.b.a. (6, E3) A vast assortment of good beers (none of that 'we serve imports: Corona and Fosters' nonsense) includes excellent Belgian and American microbrews. The bar is attractive day or night. The crowd's convivial

and there's mellow jazz at times in one room.
☎ 942-3731 ✉ 618 Frenchmen St 💲 no cover 🕑 5pm-5am Mon-Fri, 2pm-5am Sat & Sun

Dungeon (6, C5) Descend the stone stairs into this gothic lair for midnight dancing or ghoulish cocktails. Three bars and live DJs attract everyone from yuppies to bikers.
☎ 523-5530 🖥 www .originaldungeon.com ✉ 738 Toulouse St 💲 $5 🕑 midnight-late

Lafitte's Blacksmith Shop (6, D4) This historic bar tilts ever so slightly to one side. When the weather cooperates, the shuttered windows are thrown open to allow tropical breezes to penetrate the cool dark space. It feels little changed in centuries.
☎ 522-9377 ✉ 941 Bourbon St 💲 no cover 🕑 noon-3am

Le Chat Noir (5, D4)
Slick Le Chat Noir celebrates cocktails and theatrics. In the front piano bar, wide-mouthed martinis are sipped and swilled by wage slaves and other swells. The adjoining theater hosts cabaret musicals, political satire and off-color monologues.
☎ 581-5812 🖥 www .cabaretlechatnoir. com ✉ 715 St Charles Ave 💲 shows tickets $15-20; no cover for bar 🕑 7pm-late Tue-Sat; show times vary 🚋 St Charles at Julia St

Loa (5, E3) The bar of the fashionable International House Hotel, Loa is a great place to grab a daytime drink. The huge windows overlook the CBD's streetscape of dedicated worker bees. Music runs the gamut of world beats. At night everyone looks good bathed in candlelight.
☎ 553-9550 ✉ 221 Camp St $ no cover
☾ 5pm-late

Molly's at the Market (6, E4) This epicenter of the Irish expat community sponsors a raucous St Patrick's Day bash. The rest of the year, share a pint with the resident stiffs: former owner Jim Monaghan and 'Irving' reside in their respective urns behind the bar. Lots of living Quarter denizens make this their regular haunt.
☎ 525-5169 🖵 www .mollysatthemarket.com ✉ 1107 Decatur St $ no cover ☾ 10am-6am

Napoleon House (6, C5) Napoleon really missed out on a good time. Unbeknown to the exiled emperor, some scheming locals, including the mayor, wanted to rescue him from St Helena and set him up in this handsome building. He died before the plot set sail. Martial classical music and dramatic pictures of the emperor arouse the urge to have another drink. Try the Pimm's cup or a Sazerac (see boxed text, right).
☎ 524-9752 ✉ 500 Chartres St $ no cover
☾ 11am-midnight Mon-Thu, 11am-1am Fri & Sat, 11am-7pm Sun ♿

Old Absinthe House (6, C5) In the 1870s this sweaty Bourbon St fixture was one of the city's many bars serving the now outlawed absinthe, a greenish herbal liqueur. Legal stand-ins, such as Pernod or Herbsaint, still make an appearance in the absinthe frappe and other cocktails of the era. This place is always packed.
☎ 523-3181 ✉ 240 Bourbon St $ no cover
☾ 11am-late

Parasol's Restaurant & Bar (3, H4) This cheery neighborhood joint is packed day and night with folks escaping the old lady (or old man) and household chores. The bar's been there forever and has the scars to prove it. Incredible po'boys (p58).
☎ 897-5413 ✉ 2533 Constance St $ no cover
☾ 11am-10pm 🚌 cab

Pat O'Brien's (6, C4) Home of the hurricane, a dastardly strong rum punch, Pat O'Brien's has more tourist appeal than the city's art museum: these hurricanes are yummy and real ass kickers. Before you know it, you'll have consumed enough confidence juice to commandeer the piano in the inside bar. However the real magic occurs outside at the courtyard tables.
☎ 525-4823 🖵 www .patobriens.com ✉ 718 St Peter St $ no cover
☾ 10am-4am

Toast of the Town

New Orleans is not only famous for inventing a variety of cocktails, it supposedly invented the very first cocktail. In an apothecary on Royal St, the distinguished AA Peychaud mixed his patented bitters with cognac brandy in egg cups, called *coquetiers* in French, 'jiggers' in English. Eventually slurred to 'cocktail,' a new American pastime was born. In this creative spirit, the city went on to concoct or perfect other alcoholic recipes, including the following classics.

- **Hurricane** (fruit-punch mix, rum) – Pat O'Brien's (above)
- **Mint julep** (ice, mint, bourbon) – Columns Hotel (left)
- **Pimm's cup** (Pimm's, lemonade, 7-Up and a cucumber slice) – Napoleon House (left)
- **Sazerac** (whiskey, syrup, Herbsaint, Peychaud's bitters) – Sazerac Bar (p64)
- **Ramos gin fizz** (gin, sour mix, half-and-half, orange blossom water) – Sazerac Bar (p64)
- **Vieux Carré** (whiskey, cognac, sweet vermouth, Benedictine and bitters) – Carousel Bar (left)

R Bar (6, E3) A funky Faubourg Marigny bar that attracts the owners of other bars. The R stands for the 'r' in art, and owner Jonathan Ferrara (of the gallery, p43) sees the walls as his canvas. Adding to the goofy scene are underwear-clad women who read books atop the beer cooler. Upstairs there are B&B rooms – in this case it stands for 'bed & beverage.'
☎ 948-7499 ✉ 1431 Royal St 💲 no cover 🕑 3pm-late

St Joe's Bar (3, C5) Of all the houses of worship to St Alcohol, this Uptown spot is the only one offering heavenly style with a down-to-earth attitude. The front room broods with carved wooden crosses and church pews, while the back patio allows contemplation of the heavens above.
☎ 899-3749 ✉ 5535 Magazine St 💲 no cover 🕑 5pm-late 🚖 cab

Sazerac Bar (5, D2) A real classic with gorgeous art-deco murals, legend has it that the bullet-sized dent in the wall was a failed attempt on the life of Louisiana politician, Huey Long. No doubt he was drinking a highball of Sazerac or the bar's other signature drink, the Ramos gin fizz at the time. Service is smooth; business casual.
☎ 529-7111 💻 www .fairmont.com ✉ Fairmont Hotel, 123 Baronne St 💲 no cover 🕑 11am-midnight Sun-Thu, 11am-1am Fri & Sat

360 Bar (5, F3) The ear-popping elevator ride up the World Trade Center delivers you to a George Jetson–style revolving bar. The stunning view of the Mississippi is worth the price of a cocktail or two. On many nights, the bar transforms into an upscale dance club with house, techno and hip-hop DJs.

☎ 595-8900 ✉ World Trade Center, 2 Canal St 💲 DJ nights $7-10 🕑 11am-2am Mon-Wed, 11am-4am Thu-Sat

TwiRoPa (2, E3) In an old rope factory in the heart of the old Warehouse District, there are bars and stages aplenty in this 100,000-sq-ft party space. This is what passes for trendy in laid-back New Orleans. Music veers toward modern.
☎ 587-3777 💻 www .twiropa.com ✉ 1544 Tchoupitoulas St 💲 $15-20 🕑 11pm-very late 🚖 cab

Wine Loft (5, E4) This is a smooth, jazz-filled meeting spot for local professionals who plot courses through the dozens of wines available by glass. There are good hors d'oeuvres.
☎ 561-0116 ✉ 752 Tchoupitoulas St 💲 no cover 🕑 5pm-late 🚖 cab

Green with Absinthe

A 19th-century urban legend tells the story of a Northerner who visits New Orleans and stops into one of the city's many Sazerac bars. After his first drink, he announces that Sazerac is a drink with integrity. His second helps him realize that the South is incredibly misunderstood. After the third he is a converted rebel and begs the bartender for change in Confederate money.

Perhaps it was this story that cinched the prohibitionists' derogatory opinion of absinthe. A strong herbal liqueur, absinthe gained a grand following in France and New Orleans, and was traditionally served diluted with sugar or in cocktails like the Sazerac. The herbal ingredient of wormwood, not absinthe's high alcohol content, was witch-hunted for causing madness, and all wormwood products were outlawed in the USA in 1912.

The Sazerac cocktail, however, still survives today. Like an aging rock band, Sazerac just replaced washed-up ingredients with younger faces: brandy was traded for whiskey, and absinthe for Herbsaint (a locally produced anisette). Peychaud's bitters is the one surviving member.

LIVE MUSIC

Donna's Bar & Grill

(6, C4) This is one of the best scenes in New Orleans. A diverse crowd listens to excellent jazz. Well-known musicians often drop by for impromptu jam sessions. On Monday nights, there's a free feed after the first set.
☎ 596-6914 ▯ www
.donnasbarandgrill.com
✉ 800 N Rampart St
$ $7-10 ✦ 6:30pm-
late, shows at 9:30pm
Thu, Sun & Mon, 10:30pm
Fri & Sat

Funky Butt (6, C4)

The Butt is more sexy than funky, with mobster mood colors and intimate tables. Named after a Buddy Bolden tune, Funky Butt attracts the more modern edge of the jazz crowd, but straight-up swingers are still a fixture.
☎ 558-0872 ▯ www
.funkybutt.com
✉ 714 N Rampart St
$ $5-15 ✦ 7pm-late,
shows at 10pm

House of Blues (6, C6)

Legends like Dolly Parton and Etta James have played the same stage as local blues and rock talent. An annex club, The Parish, hosts smaller local acts. Sunday gospel brunches widen HOB's appeal.
☎ 310-4999 ▯ www
.hob.com ✉ 255 Decatur
St $ $8-50 ✦ 8pm-
2am, Sun gospel 9:30am-
4pm ♿ good ♨

Howlin' Wolf (5, E5)

This club started promoting local progressive-rock bands, expanded to attract national

Music with Your Eggs

Think comfort, think fun, think New Orleans. Another great local tradition is the jazz brunch on Sunday. Settle into a table, order a cocktail or three and while the courses make their way out to you, you're serenaded by a live band. Pretty soon it's 3pm and you've whiled away a wonderful day. Typical.

The following all offer Sunday brunches with live jazz. It's a popular institution, so book in advance. In the French Quarter, there's **Arnaud's Restaurant** (p49), **Cafe Sbisa** (p49) and the **Court of Two Sisters** (p50). In the Warehouse District the **Praline Connection** (p55) saves your soul with Gospel jazz while **Commander's Palace** (p56) offers the most lavish experience out in the Garden District.

groups and diversified to include jazz and blues. Look for groups like the Tragically Hip and Stroke.
☎ 529-5844 ▯ www
.howlin-wolf.com ✉ 828
S Peters St $ $5-20
✦ show times vary
🚕 cab

Jimmy Buffett's Margaritaville Cafe (6, E4)

Margaritaville is a long way from the Big Easy, isn't it? The New Orleans branch of the parrot-head cult isn't purely rampant commercialism. Jimmy

Buffet came here as a kid, and later started his music career here. Daytime bands, usually R&B and blues, are a great way to catch live music before dark.
☎ 592-2565 ▯ www
.margaritavillecafe.com
✉ 1104 Decatur St $ no
cover ✦ 9am-late; shows
at 3pm, 6pm & 9pm ♨

Le Bon Temps Roulé (3, E5)

This classic hangout draws the Tulane and Loyola crowd, as well as grittier neighborhood types. Frequent specials ($1 beers

Cram into Donna's Bar & Grill for an impromptu jam session

or free oysters on Friday) also make it as easy on the pocket. Hosts local bands four nights a week. ☎ 895-8117 ✉ 4801 Magazine St $ no cover-$5 ⏱ 4pm-late, music 9pm Wed-Sat 🚕 cab

Maple Leaf Bar (3, A1)
An incredible ensemble of local musicians hang at this legendary bar. Nightly shows of New Orleans brass, funk, ragtime and R&B go down smooth and easy. ☎ 866-9359 ✉ 8316 Oak St $ $5-10 ⏱ 3pm-late 🚕 cab

Mid-City Rock 'n' Bowl (4, A5)
This place rocks, and it really is a bowling alley. Blues, zydeco and R&B acts are at the top of their game. The Wednesday swing and

Thursday zydeco shows are staples for dancin' fanatics. ☎ 482-3133 ✉ www .rocknbowl.com ✉ 4133 S Carrollton Ave ⏱ noon-late, shows 10pm $ $5-10 🚕 cab

Palm Court Jazz Café (6, E4)
Traditional and Dixieland jazz bands play this elegant supper club. Many folks skip the food and listen to the tunes from the bar area. ☎ 525-0200 ✉ www .palmcourtcafé.com ✉ 1204 Decatur St $ $5 ⏱ 7-11pm Wed-Sat 👤

Preservation Hall (6, C4)
A veritable museum of traditional and Dixieland jazz, Preservation Hall is a pilgrimage. But like many religious obligations, it ain't

Local legend Tipitina's

necessarily easy, with no air-conditioning, limited seating and no refreshments (you can bring your own water, that's it). Get in line early to get a seat. ☎ 522-2841 ✉ www .preservationhall.com ✉ 726 St Peter St $ $5 ⏱ from 8pm

Snug Harbor (6, E3)
This swank jazz club hosts such luminaries as Jason Marsalis, R&B vocalist Charmaine Neville, and the modern jazz quartet Astral Project. Reserve tickets in advance, business casual. ☎ 949-0696 ✉ www .snugjazz.com ✉ 626 Frenchmen St $ $10-20 ⏱ shows at 9pm & 11pm

Tipitina's (3, E6)
Founded in honor of New Orleans celebrity Professor Longhair, Tipitina's was the home of 1970s R&B. Today it's got a cool mix of jazz, blues, soul and funk, and draws local and national talent. Locals love the Sunday Cajun dancing. ☎ 895-8477 ✉ www .tipitinas.com ✉ 501 Napoleon Ave $ $5-50 ⏱ usually from 7pm, from 5pm Sun 🚕 cab

Music Stars
New Orleans has so much live music that making a choice can be debilitating. Don't fret: there is so much good music that it's hard to go wrong at one of the good clubs listed in this book. Here are a few of the more notable artists worth seeking out. In a few cases they have regular gigs at a particular club.

- **Bob French & Friends** (brass) – Donna's Bar & Grill (p65), Monday
- **Charmaine Neville** (R&B vocalist) – Snug Harbor (right), Monday
- **Don Vappe** (trad jazz)
- **John Boutte** (R&B vocals)
- **Kermit Ruffins & Barbecue Swingers** (trad jazz/swing)
- **Marva Wright** (R&B vocals)
- **Rebirth Brass Band** (brass) – Maple Leaf Bar (above), Tuesday
- **Snooks Eaglin** (R&B guitar)
- **Treme Brass Band** (trad second-line brass) – Donna's Bar & Grill (p65), Friday

PERFORMING ARTS & CINEMA

Contemporary Arts Center (5, D5) The anchor for the Warehouse District's art community, the CAC sponsors modern plays, dance, performance art and films. Musical shows include both tributes and programs dedicated to cutting edge sounds. The center hosts the annual New Orleans Film Festival (usually Oct; www.new orleansfilmfest.com).
☎ 528-3805 ⬛ www .cacno.org ✉ 900 Camp St 💲 from $10 🚊 St Charles at Lee Circle ♿

Entergy IMAX Theatre (6, D6) Amazon caves, volcanoes, dolphins and much more get supersized on the 5½-storey screen in this surround-sound theater. Part of the Audubon Aquarium of the Americas complex, combination tickets are available.
☎ 581-4629 ⬛ www .auduboninstitute.org ✉ 1 Canal St 💲 $8/5 ♿

Le Petit Théâtre du Vieux Carré (6, D5) One of the oldest theater troupes in the country, Le Petit performs a variety of Southern-flavored plays. Stage-adapted fairy tales and standard musicals also fill the schedule. The theater itself is gleaming after major restoration and modernization.
☎ 522-2081 ⬛ www .lepetittheatre.com ✉ 616 St Peter St 🕑 afternoon & evening shows 💲 $20-30/10 ♿

Louisiana Philharmonic Orchestra (5, D3) Led by music director Klauspeter Seibel, the orchestra is one of only two musician-owned symphonies in the world. An instrument 'petting zoo' precedes special family programs. Performances are at the downtown 1921 Orpheum Theater (5, D2; 129 University Place), and the annual season runs from September through May.
☎ 523-6530 ⬛ www .lpomusic.com ✉ 305 Baronne St 💲 tickets $13-62, discounts for family events ♿

Louisiana Superdome (5, B3) Resembling a huge exhaust vent, the Louisiana Superdome reaches 27 stories high and encompasses 125 million cu ft of space. During the football season, the Superdome is where the New Orleans Saints play their home games. Every year, the Sugar Bowl (p61) is held here, and the NFL's Super Bowls return to the stadium an average of every four years.
☎ 587-3822 ⬛ www .superdome.com ✉ 1500 Sugar Bowl Dr

Mahalia Jackson Theatre of the Performing Arts (6, C3) Named in honor of the great gospel singer Mahalia Jackson, this theater houses the renowned New Orleans Opera Association (www.new orleansopera.org) and New Orleans Ballet Association (www.nobadance.com).
☎ 565-7470 ✉ Armstrong Park

Southern Repertory Theater (6, C6) The moody, and sometimes disturbing, stories of famous Southern playwrights, such as Tennessee Williams and Carson McCullers, virtually fall into your lap at this tiny theater of only 150 seats.
☎ 522-6545 ⬛ www .southernrep.com ✉ 3rd fl, 333 Canal Pl 💲 $23/15 ♿

Stimulate your senses at the Contemporary Arts Center

GAY & LESBIAN NEW ORLEANS

Southern Decadence

Mixing mainstream corporate sponsors with events like the legendary banana-sucking contest, **Southern Decadence** (www.southerndecadence.net) lives up to its name in every way possible. For five days, beginning at midnight the Wednesday before Labor Day weekend (the first weekend in September), upwards of 120,000 gay, lesbian, transgender and 'other' revelers converge on the Big Easy for a literal orgy of partying. The nexus of gay bars and clubs on Bourbon and St Ann Sts are ground zero, with most people partying on the sidewalk since the clubs are simply jammed.

Among the multitude of highlights is the Grand Marshall's Parade on Sunday, which starts at 2pm – an unholy hour given that many of the balls start after midnight and go until 9am.

Bourbon Pub and Parade Disco (6, D4) The party spills out onto the sidewalk at this popular dance and video club, which vies with neighboring Oz for gay dance and party biz. Constant drink specials, foam parties, female impersonators and more mayhem ensure it's raucous all the time.
☎ 529-2107 🖳 www .bourbonpub.com ✉ 801 Bourbon St 💲 free-$5 🕑 24hr

Good Friends (6, C4)
The crowd of regulars really are good friends, partly because the bar stools are so damn comfortable. Easy-on-the-eye bartenders make the bar's famous drink, the separator (Kahlúa ice cream, milk, brandy and coffee liqueur). The upstairs piano area, the 'Queen's Head Pub,' heats up with

show tunes on Sunday nights. The balcony is a good spot to chill.
☎ 566-7191 🖳 www .goodfriendsbar.com ✉ 740 Dauphine St 💲 no cover 🕑 24hr

Lafitte in Exile (6, D4)
Easily the most popular gay bar in the Quarter, Lafitte's gets a vastly mixed and friendly crowd of all ages and sexes. The upstairs balcony is one of the best and as you'd expect, the drink specials just keep coming. Stand at the ground floor

doors and watch the tourists gawking.
☎ 522-8397 🖳 www .lafittes.com ✉ 901 Bourbon St 💲 no cover 🕑 24hr

Oz (6, D4) Even Uptown debs have been seen shaking their tail feathers at this mixed dance club. The pump-and-grind area is surrounded by a cast-iron balcony and the bar is manned by buff, shirtless bartenders. In the wee hours, clothing becomes more of a concept than a reality.
☎ 593-9491 🖳 www .oznewlorleans.com ✉ 800 Bourbon St 💲 $5 🕑 24hr

Rawhide 2010 (6, C4)
Leather in the morning, leather in the evening, leather at suppertime. Behind those dark windows, you'll find well-groomed men wearing, or not wearing, leather. Break from the uniform and wear a Rawhide T-shirt and you'll get happy-hour prices around the clock.
☎ 525-8106 🖳 www .rawhide2010.com ✉ 740 Burgundy St 💲 no cover 🕑 24hr

Where everybody knows your name

SPECTATOR SPORTS

Football

The National Football League's New Orleans Saints play eight home games from August through December at the gigantic Louisiana Superdome (p67). The Saints march in but rarely march out victorious. Many fans attribute this losing streak to the Superdome's unfortunate location over an old cemetery. Several years ago, a well-respected voodoo priestess was brought in to break the curse; the antidote only lasted one game.

The hottest college football ticket is the Sugar Bowl (p61), featuring the two best college teams. In 2004, Louisiana State's Tigers made the short drive down from Baton Rouge to win the national title.

Basketball

The National Basketball Association's Hornets team, formerly located in Charlotte, North Carolina, is now looking for success in New Orleans. The season runs from October to April.

Baseball

The New Orleans Zephyrs, a minor league AAA baseball team, is affiliated with the Houston Astros, which many locals consider *their* Major League Baseball team. The baseball season runs from April to October.

Horseracing

One of North America's oldest racetracks, the Fair Grounds Race Track (see boxed text, below) hosts thoroughbred racing from Thanksgiving through March. In May, Jazz Fest (p10) turns the fair grounds into a marathon of music and merriment.

Offices & Venues

Tickets for most professional sports events are handled by **Ticketmaster** (www.ticketmaster.com).

New Orleans Saints (5, B3; ☎ 731-1700; www.neworleanssaints.com; 1500 Sugar Bowl Dr; tickets $42-80)

Sugar Bowl (5, B3; ☎ 525-8573; www.nokiasugarbowl.com; 1500 Sugar Bowl Dr; tickets from $75)

New Orleans Hornets (5, B3; ☎ 301-4000; www.nba.com/hornets; 1501 Girod St; tickets $25-100)

New Orleans Zephyrs (☎ 734-5155; www.zephyrsbaseball.com; 6000 Airline Dr, Metairie; tickets $5-10)

Fair Grounds Race Track (4, C4; ☎ 944-5515; www.fgno.com; 1751 Gentilly Blvd; tickets $1-4)

Sleeping

Greater New Orleans has over 33,000 hotel rooms; many visitors stay in the French Quarter, right on Bourbon St, although the drawback is waking up with the aftermath of the previous night's party. The Quarter's outer fringe is the best compromise: it's close, but not too close, to the action.

In the CBD and Warehouse District, chain hotels – from boutique to high-rise corporate – accommodate business travelers, conventioneers and budget-seekers (in slow times, prices are often slashed). Further upriver, the Garden District is a good base for Mardi Gras – many parades travel down St Charles Ave, where there are large hotels catering to groups and families, offering shuttle services to the Quarter and the convention center. Friendly B&Bs in galleried homes are ideal for romancing couples or business travelers escaping sterile chain hotels. Otherwise, the neighborhood, however beautiful, is a little too residential for most visitors.

Room Rates

The categories indicate the cost per night of a standard double room in high season.

Top End	$200 and up
Mid-Range	$100–199
Budget	under $99

The romantic glow of Soniat House (right)

The high demand for rooms in the Quarter ensures you won't get what you pay for: mid-range rooms are really budget quality, with well-worn furnishings and musty air-conditioning. Things improve as you move up the price scale and out of the Quarter; most hotels have interior courtyards or exterior balconies and some semblance of Old-World charm. Off-street parking typically costs $20 a day at the smaller hotels, $25 and up at the larger hotels.

One option many travelers enjoy for the space and hominess it allows is renting an apartment for a week or even a few nights. You can enjoy a quite luxurious spread in a fashionable neighborhood like the French Quarter, Faubourg Marigny and Garden District for less than $100 a night. Try the following services: **Vacation Rentals by Owner** (www.vrbo.com) and **Vacation Rentals Online** (www.vacationrentalsonline.com).

The city's high season runs from late winter to late spring; business and rates slack off in the morbidly hot summer. All hell breaks loose during special events such as Mardi Gras, Jazz Fest, the Sugar Bowl and Southern Decadence, when rates triple and vacancies shrink to near zilch.

TOP END

Fairmont Hotel (5, D2)

It's power and scandal – not furniture polish – that you smell here. This grande dame hosted Huey Long's gubernatorial bid in 1927 and later served as his refuge from Baton Rouge. The 700 rooms reek with tradition, as does the Sazerac Bar (p64).
☎ 529-7111, 800-866-5577 ⌨ www.fairmont.com ✉ 123 Baronne St ♿ ✕ Sazerac Grill ♨

Hotel Monteleone (6, C5)

The oldest and largest (568 rooms and suites!) Quarter hotel is just as handsome as when it opened in 1886. The rooms are smallish, but the location keeps people happy. A young Liberace once played (the piano) here.
☎ 523- 3341, 800-535-9595 ⌨ www.hotelmonteleone.com ✉ 214 Royal St ✕ Hunt Room Grill ♨

Loews New Orleans Hotel (5, E4)

The city's newest luxury hotel is in a stunning old steamship company skyscraper. Views are superb and the 285 rooms and suites combine spare design sensibilities with lavish use of space. Amenities include in-room broadband, lap pool and fitness center.
☎ 595-3300, 800-235-6397 ⌨ www.loewshotels.com ✉ 300 Poydras St ✕ Café Adelaide ♨

Melrose Mansion (6, D3)

Architectural Digest drooled all over this spectacular 1880s Victorian mansion –

for very good reason. The four-poster rice beds, floor-to-ceiling windows and clean masculine furnishings are all a little dizzying. But power players and celebrities seem quite at home here; maybe they just like having a Jacuzzi in their room.
☎ 944-2255 ⌨ www.melrosemansion.com ✉ 937 Esplanade Ave ✕ Marisol (p53) ♨

Omni Royal Orleans (6, C5)

An all-white marble lobby and other palatial accoutrements pay homage to the lodging's roots as a meeting place for 19th-century sugar planters. More marble appears in each of the 346 rooms' loos, and there's a rooftop pool.
☎ 529-5333, 800-843-6664 ⌨ www.omniroyalorleans.com ✉ 621 St Louis St ♿ ✕ Rib Room ♨

Soniat House (6, D4)

This restored Creole town house is perfect for a proposal or a romantic getaway. The small inn's splendor slowly unfolds as you step through the front door into a stone carriageway, leading to a green courtyard. Rooms are decorated with European antiques.
☎ 522-0570, 800-544-8808 ⌨ www.soniathouse.com ✉ 1133 Chartres St ✕ Irene's Cuisine (p50) ♨

CBD Chain Gang

On and near Canal St, supersized chain motels have filled the void left by long-extinct department stores; the accommodations are reliable and the location is convenient. They often have deals in slow periods and this is where you'll stay if you want to use frequent traveler points. Hotels include:

Hilton (5, F4; ☎ 800-445-8667; www.hilton.com; 2 Poydras St) has 1616 rooms, excellent river views

Hyatt Regency (5, C3; ☎ 800-532-1496; www.hyatt.com; cnr Loyola Ave & Poydras) has 1184 rooms, inconveniently located by the Superdome

Marriott (6, C6; ☎ 888-364-1200; www.marriott.com; 555 Canal St) has 1290 rooms, truly enormous with some good views

Ritz-Carlton (6, B5; ☎ 800-241-3333; www.ritzcarlton.com; 921 Canal St) has 452 rooms, luxurious

Sheraton (6, C6; ☎ 800-349-5406; www.sheraton.com; 500 Canal St) has 1110 rooms, vast and tall, some good views

Wyndham (5, E3; ☎ 877-999-3223; www.wyndham.com; 100 Iberville St at Canal Place) has 438 rooms, excellent river views

MID-RANGE

Andrew Jackson Hotel (6, D4) This 22-room guesthouse is a repeat favorite, mainly for its central location and friendly staff. Balconies overlook the street and the charming inner courtyard glows at night. ☎ 561-5881, 800-654-0224 ⌨ www.andrewjacksonhotel.com ✉ 919 Royal St ✕ Stella! (p52) ♿

Bourbon Orleans (6, C4) If you never want the party to end, then stay at this recently renovated nexus of mayhem. It claims to occupy the site of the famous Quadroon Balls, where quadroon beauties were introduced to white Creole aristocrats as potential mistresses. Splurge for a balcony room. ☎ 523-2222, 877-999-3223 ⌨ www.wyndham.com ✉ 717 Orleans St ✕ Café Lafayette ♿

Chateau Hotel (6, D4) It's a Herculean task to find a decent mid-range hotel in the French Quarter, but this might be it. The 45 rooms vary in size and are both clean and charming. The hotel surrounds a delightful courtyard pool. ☎ 524-9636 ⌨ www.chateauhotel.com ✉ 1001 Chartres St 🅿 free ✕ Clover Grill (p50)

Columns Hotel (3, F4) This majestic Greek Revival mansion is New Orleans' version of a country club. The exterior screams elitism, but the rooms are down to earth. The downstairs bar (p62) has a front-row view of Uptown District aristocracy. A vast Southern breakfast is included. ☎ 899-9308, 800-445-9308 ⌨ www.thecolumns.com ✉ 3811 St Charles Ave 🚋 St Charles at General Taylor St ✕ Albertine's Tea Room ♿

Cotton Exchange Hotel (5, D2) The Cotton Exchange is a comfortable hotel with a small rooftop patio and pool. The 90 rooms have broadband Internet. ☎ 962-0700, 888-211-3447 ⌨ www.cottonhotelneworleans.com ✉ 231 Carondelet St ✕ Acme Oyster House (p49) ♿

Degas House (4, C5) Edgar Degas stayed in this restored B&B when it belonged to his Creole cousins, the Mousson family. The bottom floor is a museum documenting the painter's time in New Orleans. The nine rooms are authentically decorated and well sized. ☎ 821-5009 ⌨ www.degashouse.com ✉ 2306 Esplanade Ave 🚌 48 Esplanade at Tonti St ✕ Indigo (p59) ♿

Hotel le Cirque (5, D5) This hip boutique has 148 rooms attired in citrus-colored 1960s decor – but thankfully without the attitude. Rooms are sizable and some overlook Lee Circle: close the blinds to deter that peeping general. ☎ 962-0900, 800-684-9525 ⌨ www.hotellecirque.com ✉ 2 Lee Circle 🚋 St Charles at Lee Circle ✕ Herbsaint (p54) ♿

Hotel Monaco (5, D3) How refreshing to find a corporate hotel with style: evocative of pre-WWII North Africa, the vaulted entry leads to a lobby where ceiling fans cut shadows across the marble floors. The 250 well-sized rooms come with fun accessories,

Mingle with the Uptown elite at the Columns Hotel

like faux-mink throws and complimentary goldfish. ☎ 561-0010, 866-685-8359 🖳 www.monaco-neworleans.com ✉ 333 St Charles Ave 🚋 St Charles at Poydras St 🍴 Cobalt ♿

Hotel Provincial (6, D4)
This mid-sized property in a quiet part of the Quarter has elegant period-decorated rooms. On the 5th floor you'll get a view of the Mississippi. Some of the 93 rooms have balconies overlooking the garden. ☎ 581-4995, 800-535-7922 🖳 www.hotel provincial.com ✉ 1024 Chartres St 🍴 Croissant d'Or Patisserie (p50) ♿

Hotel Villa Convento (6, D4) This family-owned and -operated hotel has bright, cheery rooms and was once a boarding house to a young Jimmy Buffet. It started life in 1833 as a Creole town house. Each of its 23 rooms are different. ☎ 522-1793 🖳 www .villaconvento.com ✉ 616 Ursulines Ave 🍴 Jimmy Buffet's Margaritaville Cafe (p65)

Lafitte Guest House (6, D4) This 1848 Creole town house has all the Old World trappings with New World friendliness. The standout rooms include No 5, with a steep spiral staircase to the loft bedroom, and No 40, occupying the entire top floor. ☎ 581-2678, 800-331-7971 🖳 www.lafitte guesthouse.com ✉ 1003 Bourbon St 🍴 Clover Grill (p50) ♿

The Cotton Exchange holding up the building next door

Maison St Charles Hotel & Suites (3, J2) This quasi-historic 130-room motel/hotel is a great place for families. Large swimming pools and courtyards give the kids lots of space to stretch their legs and lungs. A free shuttle runs to the CBD and French Quarter. ☎ 522-0187, 800-831-1783 🖳 www.maison stcharles.com ✉ 1319 St Charles Ave 🚋 St Charles at Thalia St ♿ 🍴 La Madeleine ♿

Olde Victorian Inn (6, C3) Once upon a time a Midwestern couple came to New Orleans for their honeymoon and vowed to make the city their home. Voilá: an inn is born! Proprietors Keith and André will steer first-timers to the best of the Big Easy. The four bedrooms are quasi-Victorian in style. Lemonade awaits on check-in, breakfast on arising. ☎ 522-2446, 800-725-2446 🖳 www.oldevic torianinn.com ✉ 914 N Rampart St 🍴 Donna's Bar & Grill (p65) ♿

Olivier House Hotel (6, C4) Just around the corner from the Bourbon boogie, this family-owned

hotel has 42 comfortable, versatile rooms that can sleep a duo or a big band. The courtyards, pool and friendly staff make it a good alternative to the big chains. ☎ 525-8456, 866-525-9748 🖳 www.olivier house.com ✉ 828 Toulouse St 🅿 free 🍴 Court of Two Sisters (p50) ♿

A Quarter Esplanade (6, D3) This pet-friendly hotel has modern rooms with kitchenettes, and is stumbling distance from the Quarter. The garden and pool make for a quiet refuge. ☎ 948-9328, 800-546-0076 🖳 www.quarter esplanade.com ✉ 719 Esplanade Ave 🅿 free 🍴 Marisol (p53) ♿

Queen & Crescent Hotel (5, E3) This opulent 1913 renaissance revival office building has been converted into a gem of a hotel. Each of the 196 rooms is different, but all have fine furniture and luxurious touches, such as the cotton robes. There's also a fitness center. ☎ 587-1758 800-205-7131 🖳 www.queenand crescenthotel.com ✉ 344 Camp St 🍴 Mother's Restaurant (p55)

BUDGET

Avenue Garden Hotel

(3, H3) There's a cozy courtyard in this 1897 small hotel. Rates are low and the modern rooms have a long list of amenities such as Internet access. Watch for the frequent deals that bring the prices down even more. Free continental breakfast.
☎ 521-8000, 800-379-5322 🖥 www.avenuegardenhotel.com ✉ 1509 St Charles Ave 🚋 St Charles at MLK Blvd 🏃

Sleep on a full stomach at India House Hostel

India House Hostel (4, B5)

Funky India House sports a backpacker attitude rarely found in major US cities. Solo travelers will find a network of friends and revelers hanging out by the pool, dubbed the 'India Ocean,' or in the road-weary living room. There's also a laundry on-site for those steamy nights. Evening meals are excellent and a mere $5 for all-you-can-eat. The new streetcar line is steps away.
☎ 821-1904 🖥 www.indiahousehostel.com

✉ 124 S Lopez St 🚋 Cemeteries or City Park 🍴 Liuzza's by the Track (p59)

Lamothe House Hotel

(6, E3) Shaded by the beautiful live oaks of Esplanade Ave, the 1840s-built Lamothe House wins for shabby gentility. Suites and most rooms have soaring ceilings and brooding period furnishings. Rates include a free continental breakfast and there's a free pool and a free Jacuzzi.
☎ 944-9700, 888-696-9575 🖥 www.new-orleans.org ✉ 622 Esplanade Ave 🅿 free 🍴 Coop's Place (p50) 🏃

Prytania Park Hotel

(3, J3) In the Lower Garden District, this low-key hotel offers a lot for less. It has warm honey-colored rooms in a restored 1850s guesthouse or more contemporary rooms in an adjacent motel. Kitchenettes and corporate apartments are also available.
☎ 524-0427, 888-498-7591 🖥 www.prytaniaparkhotel.com ✉ 1525 Prytania St 🚋 St Charles at MLK Blvd 🏃

Ursuline Guest House

(6, D4) The digs here are pretty straightforward: bed, door, bathroom, lamp. Any questions? Solo travelers rave about the lush courtyard rooms centered around a hot tub, and the guesthouse welcomes same-sex couples and forbids children.
☎ 525-8509, 800-654-2351 🖥 personal.msy.bellsouth.net/u/r/ursuline ✉ 708 Ursulines Ave 🍴 Mona Lisa Restaurant (p51)

Airport Hotels

Lots of flights out of New Orleans leave literally at the crack of dawn. To preserve as much sleep as possible, you may want to try one of the chain hotels out by the airport. You can catch the free shuttle to the terminal and get on your plane still half asleep. That is, if security doesn't poke you awake.

Best Western (☎ 800-528-1238; www.bestwestern.com)

Doubletree (☎ 800-222-8733; www.doubletree.com)

Hilton (☎ 800-872-5914; www.hilton.com)

Sheraton (☎ 800-325-3535; www.sheraton.com)

About New Orleans

HISTORY
In the Beginning

Records from the 18th century document small tribes of Native Americans, collectively known as Muskogeans, living along the banks of Lake Pontchartrain and the Mississippi River. Disease and war with the Europeans effectively destroyed the tribe, however alliances between escaped slaves and Native Americans were common.

Sailing into Trouble

In 1682 René Robert Cavelier La Salle traced the Mississippi from its northern beginnings to the Gulf of Mexico, claiming everything he saw for the French king, Louis XIV. For quite some time nobody really noticed or cared that La Salle named the boot-shaped wilderness at the river's end 'Louisiana.' Close to 20 years later, Pierre Le Moyne (Sieur d'Iberville) and his brother Jean-Baptiste Le Moyne (Sieur de Bienville) entered the Mississippi and founded a colony named Nouvelle Orléans. Promoting the inhospitable terrain fell to John Law, who convinced naive Germans, French and Swiss to join the crew of ex-convicts. They were joined by ships full of prisoners and prostitutes.

Spanish Order

Desperately in need of cash, the French crown ceded Louisiana to Spain in exchange for an ally against Britain. The Spanish reign in New Orleans resulted in numerous trappings of civilization being imposed, including building codes and police. The colony also absorbed French refugees, from the island of Haiti, and exiled Acadians (later known as Cajuns), from British-controlled Nova Scotia.

Reflect on times gone by at the historic Laura Plantation (p37)

Louisiana Purchase & Battle of New Orleans

In 1800 the colony passed back into the hands of France, now ruled by Napoleon Bonaparte. The US eyed the port city as an important component in western expansion. It doubled its landmass by buying the whole Louisiana territory from Napoleon for a mere $15 million. Commercially minded New England Protestants settled upriver in what is now the CBD and the Garden District, where they built ostentatious homes.

Shortly after Louisiana became a state in 1812, the US went to war with Britain. General Andrew Jackson formed an army of trained bayou runners that included Jean Lafitte, a notorious slave smuggler, to counter a British invasion of the port. The Americans trounced the Brits at the Battle of New Orleans in Chalmette (2, F3), four miles from New Orleans.

Civil War & Reconstruction

Louisiana was the sixth state to secede from the Union after the election of an antislavery president, Abraham Lincoln, in 1860. Once fighting began, New Orleans fell to the Union one year later. It would remain under military control for 15 years.

Through the 1870s, vigilante terror groups organized to thwart the federally imposed civil liberties given to the freed slaves. The new Louisiana government enforced racial segregation on public vehicles and other revocations of civil liberties. Discrimination became a sanctioned way of life.

Meanwhile, an influx of European immigrants, mainly Sicilian and Irish, poured into the city seeking economic opportunities.

New Orleans Today

Racial struggles persisted into the 20th century and beyond. Many Whites moved to the suburbs after the US government dismantled the South's segregation laws. In 1978 the city elected its first Black mayor, Ernest N Morial, ushering in a more integrated city government. In the 21st century, New Orleans continues to face challenges that have dogged it for years. It remains mostly poor and segregated by race. However, the remarkably low prices of historic homes in some of the old neighborhoods have sparked a new wave of immigrants, often artists and other creative types, who are bringing vitality to areas that have otherwise slumbered in the Southern sun for decades.

Louis Armstrong

New Orleans' beloved cornetist Louis Armstrong grew up in the area called back o' town around Liberty and Perdido Sts. At the age of 12 he was sent to reform school where he learned to play first the bugle and then the cornet. Before his musical career took off, he unloaded banana boats and delivered coal and milk. Armstrong joined King Oliver's Creole Jazz Band in Chicago in 1922 and later embarked on a solo career in New York City. In 1931 he was given a grand homecoming to New Orleans and was honored as king of the Zulus, a Mardi Gras krewe.

ENVIRONMENT

In addition to its other big city problems, such as air and water pollution, New Orleans has a difficult relationship with its watercourses – one of tenuous peace. The city's lack of elevation averages 2ft below sea level, and a series of levees and spillways thwart the water's encroachment into this natural saucer. As late as the 1940s, dense swamplands extended from the lake to the city limits acting as natural floodwalls. Most of these swamps have now been converted into subdivisions, requiring extra pumping capacity and increasing the city's vulnerability to massive flooding, should the Mississippi or Lake Pontchartrain jump their banks. Threats of hurricanes, and their potential to swamp the entire city, are taken very seriously.

GOVERNMENT & POLITICS

The state of Louisiana is organized into parishes, which are geographical units defined long ago by the Catholic Church. New Orleans falls into Orleans Parish, which is governed by an elected mayor and a city council. The government is regularly awash in scandal, and stories of unsavory deals and other schemes just keep flowing like the Mississippi.

ECONOMY

The Mississippi River has supported New Orleans since the city's birth, and the invention of the steamboat in the early 19th century ushered in the port's Golden Age. New Orleans became the commercial hub for outgoing cotton, sugar and rice, and incoming coffee, fruit and luxury goods. By 1850 New Orleans was also the largest slave-trading center in the US. During this time, the population boomed, which made New Orleans the third-largest city in the US by 1830.

In the 1960s Miami began to eclipse New Orleans as a favored

Did You Know?

- New Orleans' population is approximately 500,000
- A 'luxury' one-bedroom condo in the French Quarter costs $1500 or more per month
- New Orleans receives 11.4 million visitors per year
- French was the official language in Louisiana until 1921
- In 1945 New Orleans had 108 miles of canals (Venice has only 28 miles)

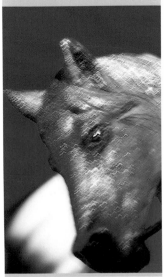

Keeping an eye on the things in the Quarter

trading partner with Latin America, and Houston took another bite out of New Orleans' shrinking shipping claims. Today, the port receives 4000 ships annually; these constitute about 15% of the total tonnage in US ports. Latin America is still its largest trade partner, and maritime-related jobs make up about 9% of the economy. New Orleans is becoming a major port for cruise ships, lured by the chance to offer vacationers packages that include time in the Big Easy. The number of annual passengers is expected to soon top one million. There are plans for a major new terminal upriver from the convention center.

Tourism is the biggest employer, with a 30% share of the economy. Oddly, tourism isn't the biggest money maker; that title goes to the oil and gas industry, which goes through almost daily boom-and-bust periods.

SOCIETY & CULTURE

New Orleanians make laid-back living deliciously enticing. Utmost on the day's list is having a good time, which usually entails food, drink and conversation. They'll talk to anyone who'll listen and will spin fantastic yarns unapologetically cloaked as history. The city abounds with so many unselfconscious eccentrics that you might wonder if you're the oddball for noticing. Even the cloistered society types are strangely democratic and remarkably outgoing.

The drawback is that nothing much gets done and rarely are people in a rush, which can be frustrating if you're waiting for a meal or a repair on a broken air-con unit. Creoles and Americans clashed over industriousness more than a hundred years ago, and the languid Creole way won – maybe there is a good reason for this.

Chugging up the mighty Mississippi

In New Orleans proper, African-Americans hold a 62% majority, with Whites comprising 35% and Hispanics 3% of the population. A large community of Southeast Asians, predominantly Vietnamese, live in the far eastern suburbs of the city. Although the distribution of power and wealth is unbalanced, the city enjoys a unique position in modern race relations thanks to the legacy of free people of color, a group composed of antebellum freed slaves and the children of mixed relationships. Free people of color owned property, were educated and practiced skilled trades long before those inalienable rights were won for everyone.

Etiquette

New Orleans is very Southern in its social etiquette. Greeting people on the street and generously dispensing 'thank-yous' and 'pleases' helps to put locals at ease. You'll receive in return lots of 'honeys' and 'sweeties' from the clerk taking your food order or the chambermaid returning home on the bus. These pleasantries help draw you into the Crescent City's ample bosom of family and friends.

ARTS
Architecture

If you hate good food and despise a good time, then New Orleans is still worth it for the architecture alone. In the Quarter, stuccoed buildings with their lacy ironwork balconies pose like mantilla-veiled Spanish maidens. These were built during the Spanish occupation and bear the initials of their first owners. Huddled in the residential section of the Quarter, the shuttered Creole town houses are more suggestive of the Caribbean than the American South, with their coral-colored facades faded by the sun. Creole cottages are constructed flush to the sidewalk, creating an impregnable fence and daring

Visual Arts

Nurtured by an atmosphere that seems to favor creativity over commerce, scores of artists call New Orleans home. Cheap rents have drawn painters, sculptors and other creative folk to artistically frayed neighborhoods such as Bywater, the Irish Channel and the Lower Garden District. The glorious results, a riot of styles and mediums, are on display in the galleries in and around Julia St in the Warehouse District and up and down Magazine St (p43).

The regenerated Warehouse District

passersby to peek through the louvered shutters. Their eaves hang over the sidewalk, sheltering people from the sun and rain. During Victorian times the austere fronts were decorated with swirling lintels and gables, like a young girl were playing dress-up with her mother's jewelry.

The simple Creole domiciles seem a bit like quaint garages compared to the totalitarian Greek Revival mansions in the Garden District and Uptown, where nouveau riche Americans built palaces in competition with each other.

Music

The brash sounds of brass instruments found an eternal home in New Orleans and were never deposed as more modern trends swept the rest of the nation. The post–Civil War marching bands first introduced the populace to the powerful belch of the tuba, the blue cry of the trumpet and the heartbeat of the bass drum. Once the brass found their way into the hands of the city's African-Americans, the result was jazz.

Two native sons are credited with rearing America's indigenous music. Cornetist Buddy Bolden steered ragtime into jazz time, and

Leisure Listening

For a brief overview of New Orleans' musical heritage, check out the following albums:

- Louis Armstrong, *Louis Armstrong 1925–1926* (Chronological Classics)
- Jelly Roll Morton, *Jelly Roll Morton 1939–1940* (Chronological Classics)
- Professor Longhair, *Collector's Choice* (Rounder, 1950s)
- Dirty Dozen Brass Band, *Voodoo* (Columbia, 1989)
- Wynton Marsalis, *Standard Time Vol: 3 The Resolution of Romance* (Sony, 1990)

Up close and personal – New Orleans style – with the Jimmy Thibodeaux Band

Louis Armstrong made it swing. A group of White musicians, called the Original Dixieland Jazz Band, smuggled the New Orleans sound out of the city to the rest of the nation in 1917.

Jazz went on to meet other musical sculptors in Memphis, Chicago, New York and Kansas City. In its hometown it stayed true to the horns, which presided over funerals, parades and cocktail parties. Even today, lanky kids outsized by their instruments play the songs of long ago with modern inflections: a little rap, a little R&B and a whole lot of soul.

Other musicians and musical styles flourished within the local cult of celebrity and a few national exports. Professor Longhair rolled out popular good-times songs on his piano. Fats Domino crooned his way to Top 40 fame. The Neville Brothers became the first family of New Orleans R&B for many decades. Wynton Marsalis has brought the music back home with his post–Miles Davis jazz. However it's not the exports that define New Orleans' vibrant music scene; it is the small-town darlings who make a living out of moving people to dance and sing.

Literature

New Orleans has been a muse to many great authors. George Washington Cable (1844–1925) found rich fodder for his fictional books *Old Creole Days* (1879) and *The Grandissimes* (1880). In *The Awakening* (1899), Kate Chopin (1851–1904) wrote about a character who discovers the malaise of the leisure class amid the Garden District's lavish homes. While living at 636 St Peter St, Tennessee Williams wrote *A Streetcar Named Desire* (1947). Walker Percy's (1916–1990) first novel, *The Moviegoer* (1961), hauntingly taps into the despair that drives New Orleans toward its incessant parties.

Quite fittingly, the most 'New Orleans' novel is a straightforward tale of the wacky citizens who make this city more than just a sweaty swamp. John Kennedy Toole's first novel *A Confederacy of Dunces* (1980), about an overweight hot dog vendor, so perfectly captures almost every segment of New Orleans society, that his characters can still be spotted on the street today.

Faulkner House bookstore (p46)

Directory

The magnetic appeal of New Orleans' tourist kitsch

ARRIVAL & DEPARTURE
Air
Most visitors arrive by plane at the city's only commercial airport, the **Louis Armstrong New Orleans International Airport** (MSY; 2, A2).

The airport is 21 miles west of the city center in the town of Kenner. A single terminal is connected to four concourses.

AIRPORT INFORMATION
General inquiries ☎ 464-0831
Car park information ☎ 464-0204

AIRPORT ACCESS
Public transportation from the airport isn't convenient. For one or two people with little time to spare, a taxi is the best bet. Shuttle buses are an option for travelers not on a tight schedule.

Shuttle
The **Airport Shuttle** (☎ 522-3500) will deliver you from the airport to your hotel for $13/26 (one-way/round-trip).

Public Bus
The **Louisiana Transit Company** (☎ 818-1077; www.jeffersontransit.org; $1.60) runs buses from the airport to Airline Hwy (US 61) and along Tulane Ave to Loyola Place in the CBD. Pick-ups are opposite Door 7 on the departure level.

Taxi
A taxi from the airport to the CBD or Quarter costs a flat rate of $28 for one or two passengers. Each additional passenger costs $12 extra.

Bus
Greyhound (☎ 800-231-2222; www.greyhound.com) is the only long-distance bus company serving the South. Buses and trains share the **Union Passenger Terminal** (5, B4; 1001 Loyola Ave).

Train
Amtrak (☎ 800-872-7245; www.amtrak.com) trains arrive at Union Passenger Terminal (above). There are three trains: the *City of New Orleans* from Memphis and Chicago; the *Crescent* from New York City, Washington, DC, and Atlanta; *Sunset Limited* from Miami to Los Angeles.

Travel Documents
PASSPORT
All foreign visitors to the USA must have a passport that's valid for at least six months longer than your intended stay in the US.

VISA
A reciprocal visa-waiver program applies to citizens of certain countries who may enter the USA for stays of 90 days or less without having to obtain a visa. Generally, citizens from Canada and much of Western Europe are part of this plan, however the situation is fluid and changes often. For the latest information, contact the US embassy in your home country or consult with the US State Department (http://travel.state.gov/visa).

RETURN/ONWARD TICKET
Foreign visitors must have a round-trip ticket that's nonrefundable in the US.

Customs & Duty Free
Non-US citizens are allowed to enter the US with $100 worth of gifts from abroad. There are restrictions on fresh fruit and flowers and a strict quarantine on animals. You must declare $10,000 or more in US or foreign cash, traveler's checks or money orders. Those over the age of 21 can bring 1L of liquor and 200 cigarettes into the USA duty free.

Left Luggage

There is 24-hour baggage storage (☎ 471-0080) available on the lower level of the airport, between baggage claims 5 and 6.

GETTING AROUND

Most neighborhoods, such as the French Quarter, are very walkable. For getting between neighborhoods, there are streetcars and buses. Cabs are a good option for off-peak hours and to get to places the streetcar doesn't run. If you are staying in New Orleans, think more than twice about a rental car. Parking is scarce and expensive.

Travel Passes

NORTA (New Orleans Regional Transit Authority; ☎ 248-3900; www.norta.com) operates the public buses and streetcars. A pass is $5/$12 for one/three days.

Streetcar

There are three streetcar lines; they are both handy and a highlight of any visit to New Orleans (p21). The St Charles streetcar does a 13.5-mile loop from Canal and Carondelet Sts uptown along St Charles Ave. The Riverfront line travels 2 miles from Esplanade Ave to the Convention Center, going past the French Market and Aquarium of the Americas. The new line along Canal St splits and goes to the cemeteries in Metairie and City Park. The latter line starts at Esplanade Ave on the river front.

Streetcars run every 6 to 10 minutes during peak times and less frequently off-peak. The St Charles line runs a 24-hour service.

Taxi

If traveling at night or alone, taxis are highly recommended. **United Cab** (☎ 522-9771) is reliable. Calls for a pick-up are usually answered promptly, but prescheduled pick-ups are subject to error. Fares from the French Quarter to the Bywater are around $8, to the Garden District $10 or more, and to Mid-City $10; add an additional $1 for more than one passenger and a 15% tip. During Jazz Fest, there is a $3 special events fare from the French Quarter to the Fair Grounds, but availability is limited.

Bus

Buses are viable options for daytime travel to Mid-City (Nos 41, 42 and 43), City Park (No 48 Esplanade), Faubourg Marigny and Bywater (No 5 Marigny/Bywater) and uptown along Magazine St (No 11 Magazine). Traveling at night to points unknown is not recommended. One-way travel is $1.25 (exact change only).

Bicycle

Bicycle rentals are available through **French Quarter Bicycles** (6, D4; ☎ 529-3136; 522 Dumaine St) for $20 per day. There are few bike lanes, so a ride can involve contending with lots of traffic.

Car & Motorcycle

Cars are convenient only if off-street parking is guaranteed and extensive travel outside the city is required. Most hotels have parking garages and charge $16 to $25 per day. However if you do need to hire a vehicle, you could try **Avis** (☎ 800-3311-1212; www.avis.com; 2024 Canal St), **Budget** (6, B5; ☎ 800-527-0700; www.budget.com; 1317 Canal St) or **Hertz** (5, F5; ☎ 800-654-3131; www.hertz.com; 901 Convention Center Blvd). If you have to park in the CBD or Quarter (really don't!), New Orleans Online (www.neworleansonline.com) has details; expect high prices.

PRACTICALITIES
Business Hours

Official business hours are 9am to 5pm Monday to Friday, with abbreviated schedules on Saturday and closures on Sunday. The French Quarter tends to keep more reliable hours and weekend openings than elsewhere in the city. Everything but bars close for Mardi Gras.

Climate & When to Go

From February to April, New Orleans' climate is at its most agreeable (64°F to 84°F or 18°C to 29°C). Summer is unfathomably hot and humid with temperatures often above 100°F (38°C); for an added dose of fun, June to October is hurricane season. Summer, however, is an inexpensive and less crowded time to visit. September and October cool down to pleasant. Christmas is an off-peak period, and the weather is unseasonably warm (45°F to 64°F or 8°C to 18°C) compared to that of northern locales.

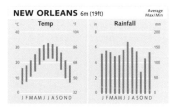

Consulates

France (5, C3; ☎ 523-5772; 1340 Poydras St)
Japan (5, C3; ☎ 529-2101; 639 Loyola Ave)
UK (5, D3; ☎ 524-4180; 321 St Charles Ave)

Disabled Travelers

All federally funded institutions are disabled-accessible by law. But historic houses are exempt, and do not have elevators or ramps. Hotels must provide wheelchair access, although accessible bathrooms are primarily found at newer properties. Wheelchair ramps or elevators are available at the ferry crossings but the Quarter is especially difficult for disabled travelers.

For details about disabled transit services, call **NORTA** (☎ 827-7433; www.norta.com). The St Charles streetcar line has not been modified to accommodate for wheelchairs.

In this book, the wheelchair-access symbol (♿) has been used to denote places with access for disabled travelers. The scale 'fair to excellent' denotes the inherent difficulties of the location.

Discounts

Admission to the city's museums and area attractions is usually discounted for children, seniors and students. Visit www.neworleans discounts.com for coupons to area attractions.

When more than one price for an attraction is listed in this book, it reflects the highest adult and the cheapest concession.

STUDENT & YOUTH CARDS

Present your student ID for discounts. As long as the little ones don't look like Britney Spears, most places will not ask parents for proof of age.

SENIORS' CARDS

Again, as long as seniors don't look like Britney Spears, they can usually claim a discount without proof of age.

Electricity

Voltage	110–115V
Frequency	60Hz
Cycle	AC
Plugs	flat two-prong

Emergencies

New Orleans' beguiling quaintness tricks tourists into thinking they are in a small village. There is a razor's edge of danger here, which requires big-city alertness.

By day you are more likely to be in well-traveled areas where muggings and other violence are less likely. If you notice you're the only one around and your instincts start to itch, heed them. Areas you should avoid on foot include the Tremé district (on the lake side of Rampart St), the Irish Channel neighborhood (on the river side of Magazine St) and deep sections of the Bywater. At night you should take a cab or drive to places outside of the Quarter.

EMERGENCY NUMBERS

Ambulance	☎ 911
Fire	☎ 911
Police (emergency)	☎ 911
Police (nonemergency)	☎ 821-2222
Rape Crisis Line	☎ 483-8888

Fitness

New Orleans isn't a workout kind of town, unless you classify moving from one air-conditioned place to another as exercise.

Most larger hotels have fitness centers, or try **Downtown Fitness Center** (5, E3; ☎ 525-2956; www .downtownfitnesscenter.com; One Canal Place, 380 Canal St; $30 per 3 days; ☯ 6am-9pm Mon-Fri). This centrally located gym has aerobics, yoga and swimming pools.

Gay & Lesbian Travelers

The gay community has a firm grip on the outer Quarter, where many businesses are gay-owned and operated. Lesbians keep a much lower profile in Faubourg Marigny and Bywater. For gay visitors, finding a place to stay, eat or party in New Orleans will not be a problem.

INFORMATION & ORGANIZATIONS

Visit the **Lesbian & Gay Community Center** (6, E3; ☎ 945-1103; www.lgccno.net; 2114 Decatur St) to get a better dish on the local landscape. **Faubourg Marigny Book Store** (6, E3; ☎ 943-9875; 600 Frenchman St) is the South's oldest gay bookstore.

Health
IMMUNIZATIONS

For most foreign visitors no immunizations are required for entry.

PRECAUTIONS

Tap water is drinkable. Be sure to drink lots of water to avoid dehydration, especially when the days are hot. Wear sunscreen and a hat and walk in the shade to avoid heat exhaustion and sunburn.

MEDICAL SERVICES

Travel insurance is advisable to cover any medical treatment you may need. Medical attention in the US is expensive, and many drugs require a prescription in the US.

Hospitals with 24-hour accident and emergency departments include the **Medical Center of Louisiana** (5, B2; ☎ 903-2311; 1532 Tulane Ave).

DENTAL SERVICES

Contact the **New Orleans Dental Association** (☎ 834-6449), which can refer you to an American Dental Association-affiliated dentist within your insurance group or at least nearby.

PHARMACIES

Walgreen's (☎ 800-289-2273) have several locations in the French Quarter and CBD.

Holidays

Jan 1	New Year's Day
3rd Mon in Jan	Martin Luther King Jr Day
3rd Mon in Feb	Presidents' Day
Feb/Mar	Mardi Gras
Mar/Apr	Easter Sunday
Last Mon in May	Memorial Day
Jul 4	Independence Day
1st Mon in Sep	Labor Day
2nd Mon in Oct	Columbus Day
Nov 11	Veteran's Day
Dec 25	Christmas Day

Imperial System

The USA stubbornly holds on to the imperial system. Gasoline is measured in US gallons. Temperatures are in degrees Fahrenheit.

TEMPERATURE
°C = (°F - 32) ÷ 1.8
°F = (°C x 1.8) + 32

DISTANCE
1in = 2.54cm
1cm = 0.39in
1m = 3.3ft = 1.1yd
1ft = 0.3m
1km = 0.62 miles
1 mile = 1.6km

WEIGHT
1kg = 2.2lb
1lb = 0.45kg
1g = 0.04oz
1oz = 28g

VOLUME
1L = 0.26 US gallons
1 US gallon = 3.8L
1L = 0.22 imperial gallons
1 imperial gallon = 4.55L

Internet

Many hotels offer Internet access, and Wi-Fi hotspots (free access) are common. Bars such as d.b.a. (p62) and Cooter Brown's (p62) also offer free access. The **Wi-Fi Directory** (www.wififreespot.com) provides a good list of Wi-Fi locations.

INTERNET SERVICE PROVIDERS

Check with your home ISP for access numbers so that you can connect to the Internet from New Orleans. If you're a client of Earthlink, dial ☎ 654-0020; for AOL dial ☎ 620-0800.

INTERNET CAFÉS

Bastille Computer Café (6, D5; ☎ 581-1150; 605 Toulouse St; per 30mins $5; ⏰ 10am-11pm)

Contemporary Arts Center (5, D5; ☎ 523-0990; 900 Camp St; 30min free with café purchase; ⏰ 11am-5pm)

USEFUL SITES

The Lonely Planet website (www.lonelyplanet.com) offers a speedy link to many of New Orleans' websites.

Jazz Fest (www.nojazzfest.com)

New Orleans Online (www.neworleansonline.com)

Offbeat Magazine (www.offbeat.com)

Times-Picayune (www.nolalive.com)

WWOZ Radio (www.wwoz.org) Has great links.

Lost Property

Call NORTA's office (☎ 248-3900) to report lost items.

Money

CURRENCY

The US dollar is divided into 100 cents (¢) with coins in denominations of 1¢ (penny), 5¢ (nickel), 10¢ (dime), 25¢ (quarter) and the relatively rare 50¢ (half dollar). Quarters are the most commonly used coins in vending machines and parking meters. Bills come in denominations of $1, $2, $5, $10, $20, $50 and $100.

TRAVELER'S CHECKS

You don't have to go to a bank to cash traveler's checks; most places accept them as cash.

CREDIT CARDS

Most major credit cards are widely accepted. The most commonly accepted cards are Visa, MasterCard and American Express.

For 24-hour card cancellations or assistance, call the following:

American Express   ☎ 800-528-4800
MasterCard   ☎ 800-826-2181
Visa   ☎ 800-336-8472

ATMS

You can easily obtain cash with a debit or credit card bearing Visa, MasterCard, Plus or Cirrus logos from ATMs all over New Orleans. The advantage of using ATMs is that you avoid paying the usual 1% commission on traveler's checks, and if you're a foreigner, you receive a better exchange rate.

CHANGING MONEY

At the airport, **Travelex** (☎ 465-9647) and **Whitney National Bank** (☎ 838-6492) change money. Better exchange rates are generally available in the CBD at the **Hibernia National Bank** (5, D3; ☎ 533-5712; 313 Carondelet St).

Newspapers & Magazines

New Orleans' only daily newspaper, the *Times-Picayune,* costs 50¢ Monday to Saturday and $1.50 on Sunday. Don't miss Friday's Lagniappe entertainment guide.

For entertainment listings, try the free weekly newspaper *Gambit*. The free monthly *Offbeat* magazine provides a complete entertainment calendar with good reviews.

Photography & Video

Luggage is now subject to high-impact X-rays, so pack any film and video equipment in your carry-on luggage. The **Liberty Camera Center** (5, D3; ☎ 523-6252; 337 Carondelet St) offers quick color printing and E-6 slide processing.

Walgreen's (p86) does film and digital printing.

The US uses the NTSC video system, which is incompatible with the PAL (UK and Australasia) and SECAM (Western Europe) formats.

Post

New Orleans' **main post office** (5, B4; ☎ 589-1706; 701 Loyola Ave;) is located near City Hall. Smaller branches include the **Airport Mail Center** (2, A2; in the passenger terminal), the **French Quarter post office** (6, B5; ☎ 525-4896; 1022 Iberville St) and the **CBD post office** (5, D4; ☎ 581-1039; 610 S Maestri Place) at Lafayette Square.

POSTAL RATES

Postal rates frequently increase, but at the time of writing, the rates were 37¢ for first-class mail within the USA for letters up to 1oz (23¢ for each additional ounce) and 23¢ for postcards.

International airmail to Canada and Mexico costs 60¢ for a 1oz letter and 50¢ for a postcard. For mail going elsewhere in the world, it will cost 80¢ for a 1oz letter and 70¢ for a postcard. Aerogrammes cost 70¢.

Radio

The fabulous WWOZ-FM 90.7 offers jazz, with a mix of blues, R&B and Cajun. Listen on the Internet at www.wwoz.org.

WWNO-FM 89.9 is the city's only National Public Radio affiliate, offering morning and evening news programs.

Telephone

Local calls from a pay phone generally cost 50¢.

PHONE CARDS

Phone cards are readily sold at newsstands and pharmacies.

CELL PHONES

The USA uses a variety of cell (mobile) phone systems, only one of which is compatible with systems used outside North America. Check with your provider to determine whether your phone will work.

COUNTRY & CITY CODES

USA	☎ 1
New Orleans	☎ 504
Australia	☎ 61
Japan	☎ 81
New Zealand	☎ 64
South Africa	☎ 27
UK	☎ 44

USEFUL PHONE NUMBERS

Local directory inquiries	☎ 411
International direct-dial code	☎ 011
International directory inquiries	☎ 412-555-1515
International operator	☎ 0
Reverse-collect (charge)	☎ 0
Time	☎ 529-6111
Weather/hurricane	☎ 800-672-6124

Television

Broadcast and cable channels are available in most hotels.

Time

New Orleans Standard Time is six hours behind GMT/UTC. Daylight-savings time comes into force on the first Sunday of April, when clocks are advanced one hour, and ends the last Sunday of October, when they retreat one hour.

Tipping

Tipping is not really optional in the USA. In bars and restaurants, the waitstaff are paid minimal wages and rely upon tips for their livelihoods. Tip at least 15% of the bill, or 20% if the service is great. You needn't tip at fast-food restaurants or self-serve cafeterias. Leave a dollar in the tip jar every time you buy a drink at a bar.

Taxi drivers expect a 15% tip. At top-end hotels, tip the porters $1 per bag; smaller services (holding the taxi door open for you) might justify only $1. Leave $2 behind for the housecleaning staff. Valet parking is worth about $2, to be given when your car is returned.

Toilets

Public toilets are rare in the Quarter. Two have been spotted at the Jackson Brewery Mall (6, D5; 620 Decatur St) and the French Market (6, E4). However lots of restaurants and bars are happy to have you as a patron, even if the obligatory drink is only an excuse.

Tourist Information

For information about New Orleans before you travel, the best sources are those listed under Internet (p87).

LOCAL TOURIST INFORMATION

The **New Orleans Welcome Center** (6, D4; ☎ 566-5031; 529 St Ann St; ☯ 9am-5pm) has maps and other tourist information. For material on New Orleans culture, including walking tours, try the **New Orleans Metropolitan Convention & Visitors Bureau** (3, H3; ☎ 566-5011; www.neworleanscvb.com; 2020 St Charles Ave; ☯ 8:30-5pm Mon-Sat, 10am-4pm Sun).

For excellent tours, displays and publications about parks in and around New Orleans, make sure you don't miss stopping at the **National Park Service French Quarter Visitor Center** (6, D5; ☎ 589-2636; 419 Decatur St; free; ☯ 9am-5pm).

Women Travelers

Women will feel perfectly safe traveling solo by day. But in bars and clubs, the city's natural friendliness can quickly erode into unwanted advances. Use Southern manners to deflect the liquid-courage crowd. See p86 for more information about safety.

Tampons and contraceptives are widely available. Birth control pills require a prescription. **Planned Parenthood** (3, F5; ☎ 897-9200; 4018 Magazine St) provides health services for women.

LANGUAGE

New Orleanians speak English, kind of. French heritage has left a lot of foreign terms in the local lexicon as well as imparted a Gallic spin on pronunciation. The New Orleans accent is unique, at times sounding more like a Brooklyn laborer than a Deep South belle. The accent reflects the influences of the Irish, Italian and German immigrants.

Below is a list of terms you may come across.

andouille – (ahn-*doo*-we) in France it is a sausage made with tripe; Creole versions are ground pork in casings made from smoked pig intestines

beignet – (ben-*yea*) New Orleans' version of the doughnut

boudin – Cajun sausage filled with pork, pork liver and rice

chenier – a ridge formed above swamp deposits, typically covered with live oaks

étouffée – (ay-too-*fay*) a spicy tomato-based stew that typically includes either crawfish, shrimp or chicken and is served with rice

filé – ground sassafras leaves used to thicken sauces; a Native American contribution to Louisiana cuisine

Grand Dérangement – the great dispersal of Acadians; following the 18th-century colonial wars between England and France, about 10,000 Acadians were deported from Nova Scotia by the English in 1755

gris-gris – objects having curative, protective or evil powers, used in voodoo

lagniappe – a small gift from a merchant or resident

mirliton – an indigenous vegetable with a hard shell that is cooked like squash and stuffed with either ham or shrimp and a spicy dressing

muffuletta – Italian dock workers were once sustained with this enormous sandwich of ham, hard salami, provolone and olive salad piled onto a loaf of bread

picayune – used to refer to something of little value; a coin formerly used by the Spanish in the South

rémoulade – (reh-moo-*laud*) a mayonnaise-based sauce with a variety of ingredients such as pickles, herbs, capers and mustard; crawfish or shrimp rémoulade is often a cold noodle salad

réveillon – a traditional Creole Christmas eve dinner

second line – the partying group that follows parading musicians

y'at – a term applying to those with heavy New Orleans accents; these people say the greeting, 'Where y'at?' using a very broad 'a'

zydeco – fast, syncopated Creole dance music influenced by Cajun, Afro-American and Afro-Caribbean cultures; often a combination of R&B and Cajun with French lyrics

Index

EATING

SLEEPING

SHOPPING

Sights Index

FEATURES

Irene's Cuisine	*Eating*
House of Blues	*Entertainment*
Lafitte in Exile	*Drinking*
St Louis Cathedral	*Highlights*
La Belle Galerie	*Shopping*
Galier House Museum	*Sights/Activities*
Chateau Hotel	*Sleeping*

AREAS

	Building
	Land
	Mall
	Other Area
	Park/Cemetery
	Sports
	Urban

HYDROGRAPHY

	River, Creek
	Canal
	Water

BOUNDARIES

	International

ROUTES

	Freeway
	Primary Road
	Secondary Road
	Tertiary Road
	Lane
	One-Way Street
	Mall/Steps
	Tunnel
	Walking Path
	Walking Trail/Track
	Walking Tour

TRANSPORT

	Airport, Airfield
	Bus Route
	Ferry
	Rail
	Tram

SYMBOLS

	Bank, ATM
	Christian
	Embassy, Consulate
	Hospital, Clinic
	Information
	Internet Access
	Point of Interest
	Police Station
	Post Office
	Zoo, Bird Sanctuary

24/7 travel advice

www.lonelyplanet.com